Custom Woven Interiors
Bringing color and design home with Rep weave

Kelly Marshall
with **Amy Egenberger**

Photography by John Abernathy

© 2012

CONTENTS

Introduction 1
Chapter 1: Inspiration and Design 9
Chapter 2: Materials and Tools 27
Chapter 3: Techniques and Tips 35
Chapter 4: Projects 45
    Queen Size Spread & Pillow Shams, Throw Blanket . 47
    Bedroom Rugs & Pillows 51
    Bedroom Table Runner 54
    Kitchen Rugs 57
    Dishtowels 60
    Bathroom Rug 65
    Living Room Rug, Upholstery & Pillows 68
    Self-closing Tote Bag 72
    Dining Room Table Runner & Placemats 79
    Entry Rug 83

    Garden Room Blue Rug 86
    Garden Sofa Upholstery & Rug 91
    Garden Sofa Pillows & Rug 95
    Garden Room Red Rug 99
    Garden Room Red Sofa & Pillows 103
    Garden Room Curtain & Throw 106
    Garden Room Throw 111
    Porch Table Runner & Placemats 114

Project Color Charts 119
How to Read the Threading Draft 123
Calculating Warp and Weft 124
Yarn Sources 126
Acknowlegdements 128
About the Author 129

My couch started from a sweater. I was in heaven one day, as only a weaver could be, absorbed in looking through thousands of archived weaving samples in the Högbo Textile Museum in Sandvicken, Sweden. One circular pattern in particular grabbed me and I quickly pencil-sketched it onto graph paper that landed in my folder of "someday-designs" where it waited patiently for its time. Fast-forward ten years, and I am at a museum exhibit in Minnesota that featured Oleana sweaters. A vivid red rose design of a knit sweater caught my eye and immediately spoke to my heart as a new weaving design. As I began imagining the beautiful colors and the rose pattern as Rep weave, that long-ago circular design sketch came to my mind. The perfect combination of color and pattern for the new upholstery to cover my couch in the garden room!

Welcome

Weaving has always been the artistic template that draws me in, a place where I find myself most comfortable, inspired, and at home. There is something seductive and meditative in the geometry that informs this art and compels me to weave. By sharing my experience and giving you a glimpse into the creative details behind my designs, it is my hope that this book will inspire you to explore your own creativity with color, pattern, and texture through the Rep weave process.

The textiles featured here for you are functional works of art for the home. From rugs, runners, upholstery and pillow fabrics, to towels, curtains, throws, and bed coverings, I love both the versatility and utility of woven creations possible with Rep weave. Initially, I was drawn to the graphic quality of this technique in the Scandinavian patterns and appreciated the crispness of the finished textile. I have found that graphic elements in Rep weave are easily translated to other design styles. You'll see examples and detailed instructions of many variations I have explored and found successful over the years.

Whether you are an experienced weaver, just getting started, or simply curious about one artist's creative approach, I invite you to let these pages incite your creativity as well. For that purpose, I welcome you behind the scenes of my design process that is rooted in timeless textile traditions and expressed to enhance contemporary environments.

Origins

I come from a long line of "makers." One grandmother made hats for a living, and the other was a seamstress who also knitted and crocheted. Being in the presence of their creative energy taught me at a very young age that making things is a wonderful way to use your time. They showed me the value of making something of beauty by hand that serves a practical everyday purpose, plus, as artisans they modeled for me the possibility of making a livelihood from my craft. So, as a maker, I become intrigued by the challenge of filling a need, get inspired to create something of beauty, and feel energized to bring hands, head, and heart to the task until the creation comes to life.

First, I may notice a need. Perhaps the windows could use curtains, or the bench by the back door needs a cover. Then I simply ask, what would be fun? What do I want? I start to get a sense for the function, the look, the feel, the impact I want as a result, and that leads me to the question of technique. How's that going to work? I start mapping out the project, circling back through these same criteria of fun, function, and feasibility until the concept can be translated into the texture of a woven piece.

All of the textiles in this book were designed for and woven with affection for my home. Built in 1923, this 512 square foot alley house is nestled in a quiet urban neighborhood in the upper Midwest. My neighbors and I have often chatted and wondered as to why there are so many of these small, charming houses lining the alleys. Built for soldiers returning home from World War I, these small structures sprung up in the back of each lot with the intention that a larger home would be constructed on the front portion of land when the homeowner became more established.

Because I've been doing this for many years, you might think it would be a snap to design textiles for my own home. Since Custom Woven Interiors opened for business in 1992, I've been weaving custom designed textiles for

residential and corporate settings. I work regularly with interior designers, architects, art consultants, and private homeowners to create the perfect textile for the desired purpose and location. But in my own home, there were many design decisions that I needed to make, considering my personal vision along with the flow and feel of the entire space. The creative challenge was on.

What is delightful and unique about my home is that each room can be seen from all the others. While I'm chopping carrots in the kitchen, I can look up and enjoy the beauty of my bedspread, visit with friends in the living room, and watch the birds out the dining room window, all from the same spot. The complexity enters in then, because designing for one room literally means designing for the whole house.

Getting Started

I decided to start with the bedroom, the most important room for me to have the right atmosphere: peaceful, restful, and happy. Color came first, influenced by the soft, warm honey-colored maple trim on the inside of the house next to butter yellow walls and a subdued blue paint from across the room. For the bedspread I chose subtle turquoise blues and olive greens complemented with warm browns, yellow, and a touch of dusty pink. I was often teased when I was in weaving school that everything I made had pink in it, so of course this choice made me smile. When the bedspread was first completed, I loved the design and pattern proportion but was disappointed in the colors that turned out too grayed for this part of the house. So, I remade the spread. In the same design I brightened up the colors keeping them quiet yet cheery, and this color combination gave me the "home-base" palette to reference all the other colors in the house. The colors from the bedcover spilled over into the bedroom rugs, and I added some deeper tones of red, green, and brown which are reflected in the adjacent rooms.

In the kitchen, with color still in the forefront, I deepened all the tones from the bedroom to make the rugs rich and vibrant reds, greens, turquoise, and salmon that worked well with the rusty orange walls in the back hall. The grayed tones migrated to the bathroom and picked up the hue of the steel blue cabinet. I pulled the brick red along with orange and turquoise from the kitchen rugs into the entry, and then pushed the intensity of the red into a poppy red orange with olive green for the *Oleana* sofa, rugs, and curtains in the outer garden room. There the rich turquoise in the *Patchwork* carpet by the door provided the perfect complement. The same fiery red, green, and blue are even carried out to the screened-in porch and work well with the rusted antique metal table and chairs. So, even in a small house where most of the rooms are seen in the same glance, you can design with bright to subdued, beige to poppy red, and appreciate them all together.

Chapter 1:
Inspiration and Design

Along with color, I look at catalogs and books with an emphasis on design for inspiration. Pattern and color combinations in traditional crafts, textiles, and architecture often catch my attention. Stained glass windows, iron gates, fabric samples, paintings, or wallpaper, for example, offer starting elements to the weaving.

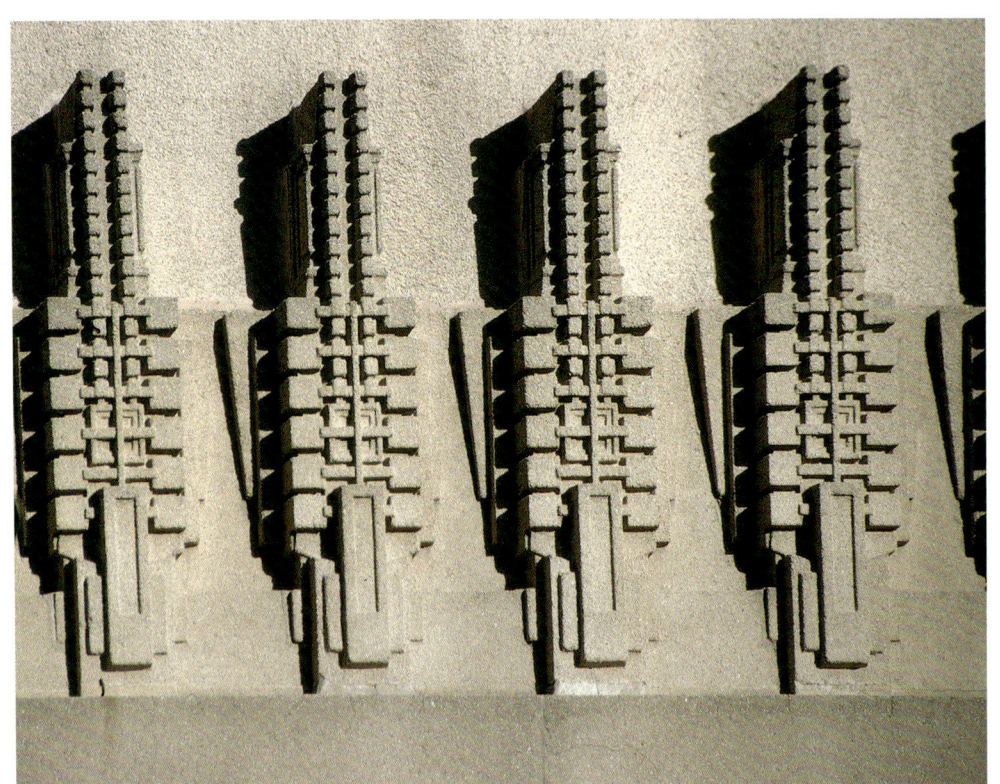 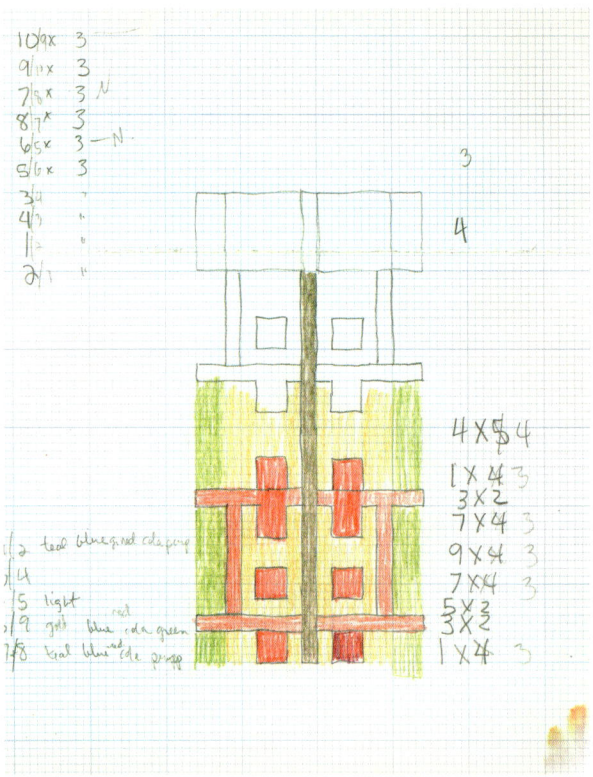

Architecture-Inspired Patterns

While leafing through an architecture book, hunting for some ideas, I spied a photograph of the cement work in Frank Lloyd Wright's "Hollyhock House" in Los Angeles, CA. I sketched the design on graph paper adding pattern blocks between motifs, then pulled in the desired colors to the design. This design, now called *Urban*, has been a favorite for many years and its regular repeat has worked well in rugs and fabric for upholstery and pillows.

I research other architectural elements from the Arts & Crafts period and have discovered numerous patterns in brick masonry, ironwork, stained glass windows, and woodwork. Even dishware and lighting fixtures reflect linear designs that translate well to the Rep weave structure. The graphic, linear characteristics of stained glass, for instance, parallel the grid-like structure of a loom with the warp and weft crossing like the lead came in a window.

Try extracting a motif from such architectural elements, repeating it, and then adding outlines or squares to fill in the design and see new patterns unfold.

So that you can get a sense of this design evolution, below are four sketches showing the developmental progression of the *Beyond* design in the living room rug.

It began as a line drawing inspired from a stained glass window I saw in a Frank Lloyd Wright house. The next sketch shows the rug that transpired from the drawing. From the desire to add more movement and color to the pattern, the next rug evolved without adding to the number of shafts and treadles. In the fourth sketch, the dark horizontal lines are achieved by reversing part of the design from the back to the front. In Rep weave, the front and back can be very different. I usually design on one side and the other just happens, but in this case, I pulled the design from the back to the front to make the horizontal lines on the front of the rug. If you remember that you can only have two colors in any vertical row, one on the front and one on the back at any given time, it is easy to figure out what the back side will look like. The *Beyond* rug for the living room was reduced, almost to half of the pattern to make the narrow runner in front of the sofa (pg. 69).

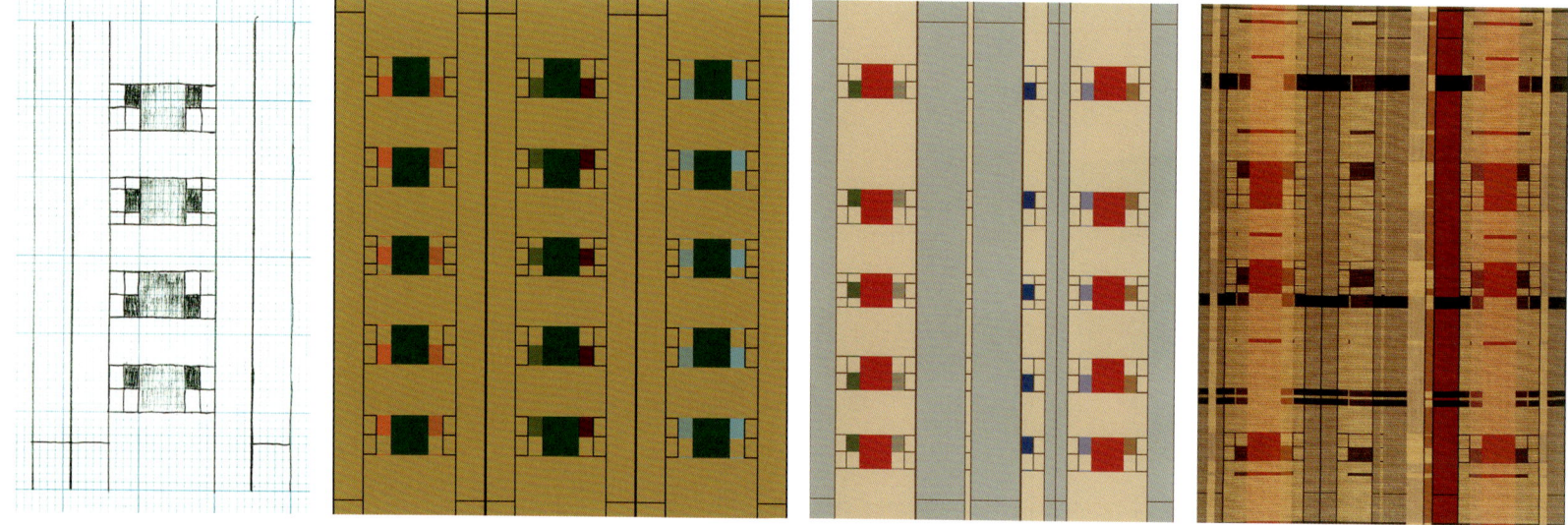

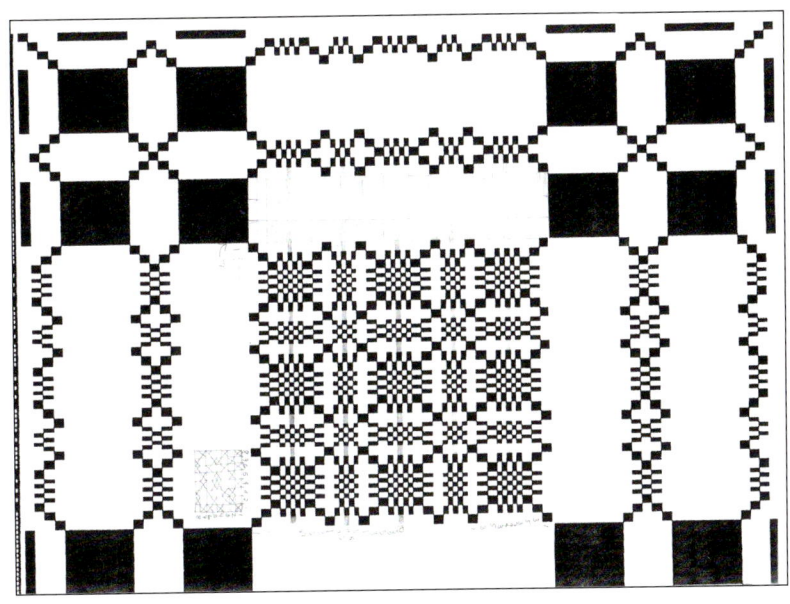
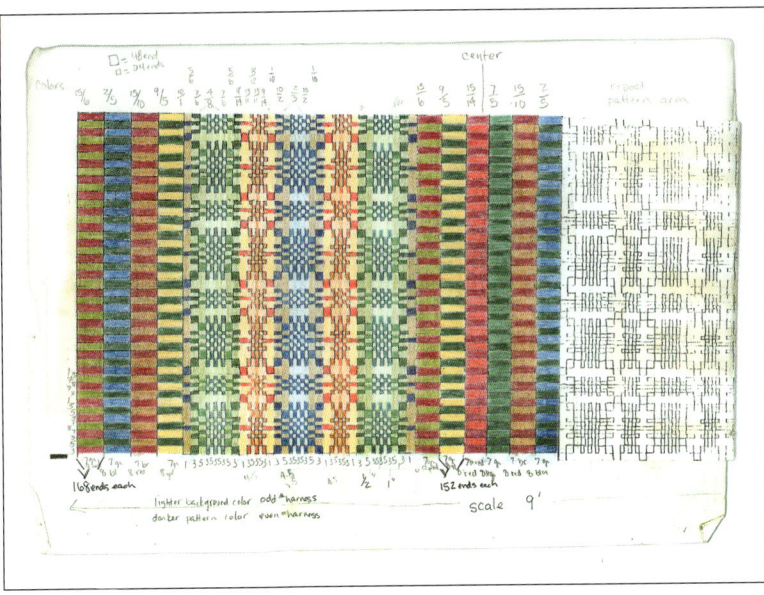

Textile-Inspired Designs

In the beginning of my career, my designs were greatly influenced by my college textile studies in Sweden. I loved to explore old coverlets and traditional weaving patterns that were usually woven in two contrasting colors like red and white or blue and white. I would arrange the pattern to fit the size needed and then start adding colors to the design, sometimes indulging in as many as thirty colors in one rug. With all these alterations, sometimes it is difficult to identify the original pattern in the final piece, as in the *Traditions* design on this page that evolved from beginning sketch to the finished textile.

You can see other examples of reworking a traditional textile in the garden room. The *Patchwork* design started from a picture of a familiar blue and white snowflake pattern that I tore out of a magazine while visiting Sweden.

I first created it in its original blue and white form. How could I translate this classic design to a more contemporary feel? I opened up a blank grid page on the computer and started filling in the squares to re-create the original image. From there, I deleted the intricate border and replaced it with a streamlined solid border and proceeded to add twelve vibrant colors to the rug. To update the wicker sofa, I selected the *Patchwork* design in a very small scale with many colors for the seat cushions and contrasted that with a large scale pattern using only three of the colors for the pillows (pg. 90). Playing with scale and color this way transforms the traditional designs to a contemporary setting.

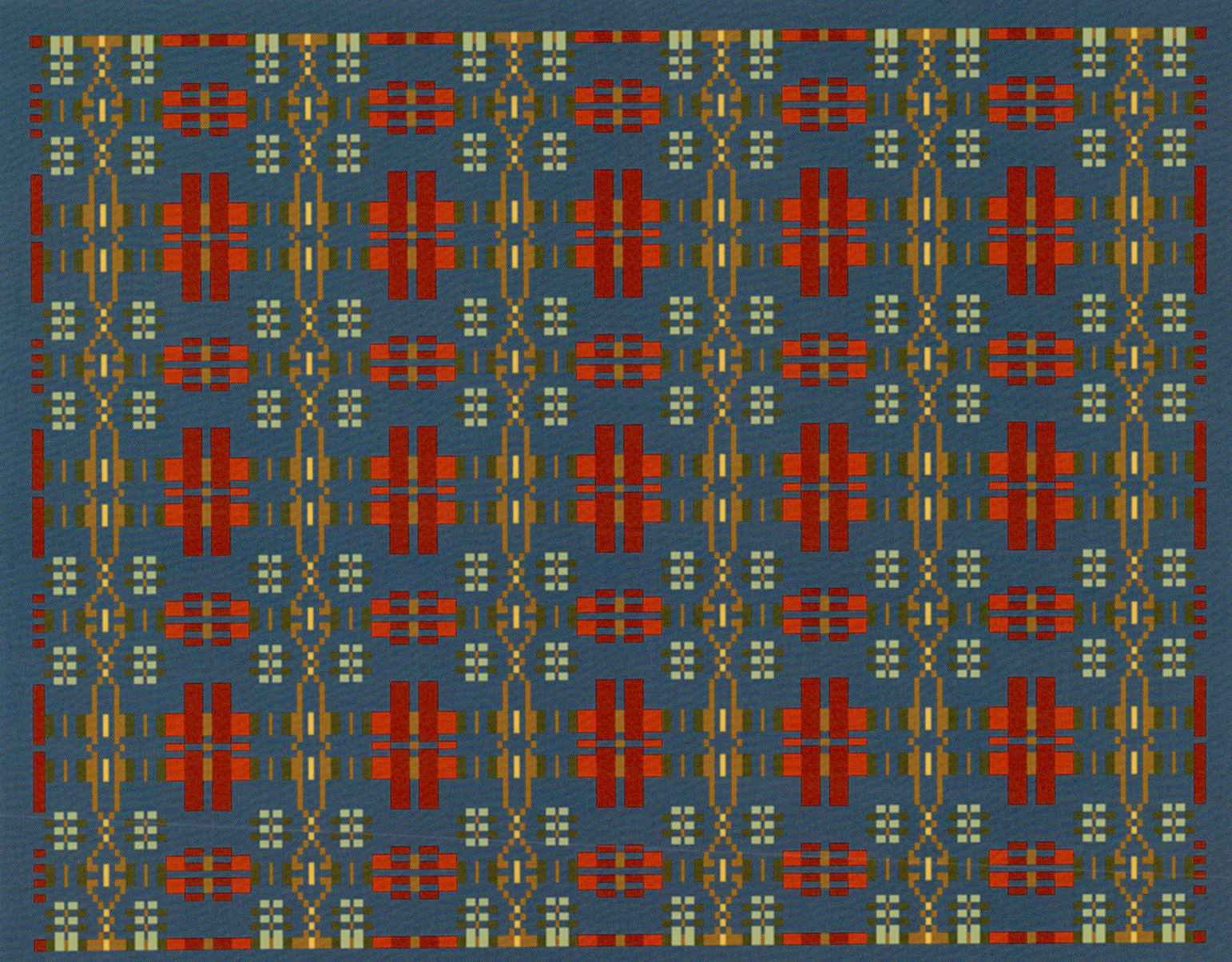

Inspiration can come from all sorts of textiles. Big poppy-red roses knitted on a deep burgundy background, with accent colors of chartreuse, plum, and sky blue on the sweater cuffs and collar, sparked the idea for my *Oleana* pattern. The rug, sofa, pillows, and curtains in the garden room (pg. 99) all got their inspiration from a particular *Oleana* sweater that I saw in a collection exhibited at the University of Minnesota College of Design, Goldstein Gallery, in 2004.

I loved the big red flowers and wanted to find a pattern with circles in it to represent these flowers. In my file of design sketches I found a rendering of a pattern with circles from Leksand, Sweden called the *Förenklad dräl*.

I liked the color proportions in the sweater, predominantly reds with the other colors as accents. So, when I started adding colors to the design, I kept large areas of reds and gathered the other colors together in limited areas for a strong contrast and a big statement of bright green down the center of the rug and sofa. To balance the activity in the colorful rug, the blanket and curtains are more subdued, keeping large areas of tone-on-tone red with limited influence of accent colors in the borders.

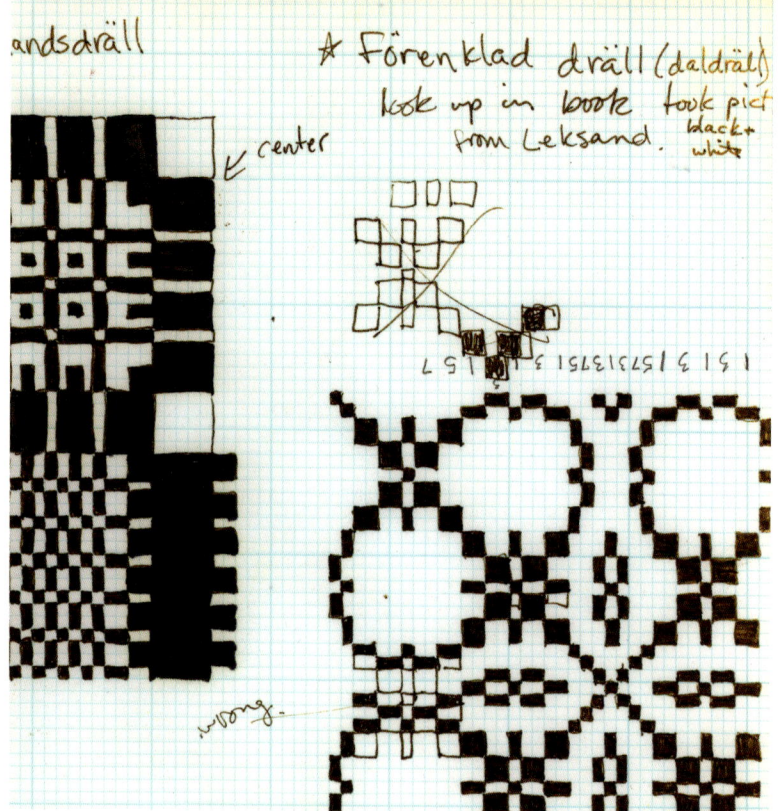

The *Oleana* pattern shows up again in the bedroom rugs where I modified the design by omitting the criss-cross detail and by emphasizing the geometric circular motifs to modernize the style. This design colorway was influenced by a rug I saw in a Garnet Hill catalog. The perfect combination of hues to tie together the bed coverings with colors in the adjacent rooms.

Both the pattern and colors of upholstery fabric often inspire my line of contemporary designs. As an example, the *Conservatory* pattern that you can see in the kitchen as a table runner and placemats as well as in the bathroom as a rug, originated from a flowery fabric on a client's sofa.

Because Rep weave is limited to linear designs, I extracted the grid-like background pattern and the luscious colors from the fabric to create the rug design for this client.

The design in the fabric is small in proportion, so I chose to make the rug pattern larger for contrast but kept the details of the lines small to reflect the smaller details of the fabric. It is easy to find enticing color combinations in this fabric, and notice how one color is portrayed by multiple colored threads used side by side. You can look closely to identify each thread individually and then see how the colors blend when it is viewed from a distance.

Designing with Color

The way colors play off one another inspires me to no end. They can create movement within a piece and magically set a mood in a room. I love gazing at the wall of yarn cones and picking colors to make the yarn wrap samples when I start a new design. My palette begins with many more colors than are needed in a piece, just so I have choices to play with while I am building color into the design. I jostle the yarn samples around to try different colors next to each other, often running to the yarn shelf for more samples to throw in a splash of new color while working on a design. When it comes to choosing color combinations that are attractive, note the intensity, value, and proportions of the colors. Over the years I have discovered that, of course, there are colors that I like better than others, but given the right proportions and combinations, all colors have a place.

Like magnets attracting or repelling one another, colors may bounce around a bit throughout my process until they find their place in the design. Some colors look great with a certain color next to them, but may clash, compete, or fight next to other colors in the same piece. So, rather than eliminating colors, I surround the odd colors with compatible hues that complement them, keeping them separate from the competing colors. This takes advantage of the vibration but allows for harmony within the piece as a whole.

Energy created by this tension adds life to the textile. For example, in the *Beyond* living room rug, the dark red, brown, and bronze green work well together and on the other side of the rug the rust, yellow, and light olive green are compatible. The light olive green and yellow are not compatible next to the dark red. It is the beige, grey, and chocolate brown that create the neutral ground that allows all the colors to work together.

When working with bright and intense colors, I always add a grounding more neutral color, like a grey, golden beige, dark maroon, or deep brown that balances and enhances the bold colors. It's almost like a dance with some crescendos of excitement and a beautiful melody of the background tone that unifies the whole piece.

In the *Flash* design (below left), the taupe background color grounds the bright primary colors. In the *Pinwheel* design (below) the maroon and wheat colors allow the brights to shine without being gaudy.

I enjoy working with patterns that are asymmetrical and often use color to balance the pattern. For instance, if a pattern is heavier on one side, I will add a strong color to the other side to draw the eye across the whole piece. Going back to the *Beyond* pattern (above left), the red stripe and block on the right are balanced by the large rust square on the left. The contrasting single patch of yellow works as a focal point near the center of the piece.

Sometimes I use an accent color in a small amount to move the eye to another area but not to make a big statement. In the *Conservatory* bathroom rug (above right), the sparks of yellow create movement around the surface of the rug.

Even in a pattern that is symmetrical, I may vary the colors from side to side to give the pattern interest and movement rather than reading a continuous repeat in one quick glance. The *Urban* (top left) design demonstrates this with varying colors from side to side.

The kitchen *Pinwheel* (top right) design is symmetrical from left to right but the color changes add excitement. The matching borders bring continuity and the dark maroon inner border defines the space around the boldly different green and salmon center halves.

The *Evolve* entry rug (right) is an example of a pattern that appears symmetrical with a strong radiating center motif, but on close inspection you'll notice that it is not symmetrical in color or pattern. These subtle differences add interest to the design.

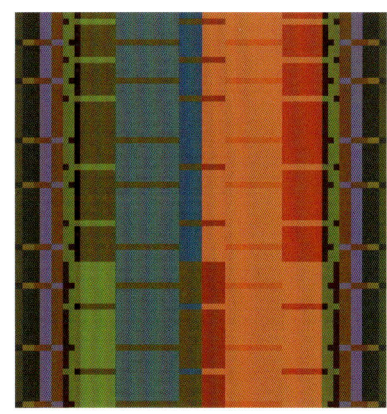

All Kinds of Input

You may discover that your own design choices flow from step to step, conversing back and forth until color, pattern, and proportion settle in and you are ready to commit your project to the loom. I enjoy weaving custom designs and working with my clients to create the perfect textile for their setting. It is fun to get design input from my clients, and we often banter back and forth with ideas and how to incorporate them into the weaving. They bring fresh ideas without knowing the restrictions of the weave structure, challenging me to put it all together. Although the Rep weave structure has several limitations, which I will discuss in the Techniques and Tips chapter, I find the possibilities for design endless through materials, pattern, and color choices.

Design to Loom

When I start designing a pattern, I always keep in mind the number of shafts. One of the challenges of the Rep technique is that it can use many shafts quickly, so it is fun to think of different ways of varying the pattern without adding more shafts. I often repeat the pattern or dissect a section of it to use separately, or I vary the quantities of smaller and larger pattern areas, or reverse a pattern for different effects without using more shafts than I have available. Using a computer and a weaving program is very helpful in this process. Any program that gives you a grid and color options will work.

Once I pick the pattern and have a sense of how many colors I need, I often select the palette from the existing room decor. My hands get busy winding the yarn threads over a one-inch piece of cardboard making a yarn wrap. I always wind two threads together at a time because they will be wound as a pair in the warp and threaded as a pair through the heddle. Each color in the pattern is made up of two threads that can be the same color or two different ones. This blending of thread colors adds depth and movement in the woven piece and allows for countless shades and variations. You create a subtle and harmonious effect if the two threads are close in value, or an energizing discord if the colors are a strong contrast.

Chapter 2: Materials and Tools

Yarn

Cotton is the fiber of choice for all the projects in this book. Because the Rep weave technique lends itself well to functional textiles, I choose cotton for its durability. These home textiles are meant to be enjoyed and used in the flow of daily living, so it is important that they can be easily washed and maintained.

Not only is cotton easy to care for, it has become the economical choice. Traditionally Scandinavian Rep weave rugs were made from linen yarns and used only for special occasions. When cotton became more readily available and affordable in the mid 1800s, Rep weave cotton rugs became more prevalent.

Warp

A 5/2 mercerized cotton is delightfully soft and has a beautiful sheen, ideal for the warp in nearly all the projects presented here. The only exception is the dishtowel which calls for more absorbency present in an 8/2 unmercerized cotton. I also like the unmercerized yarn in the dishtowels for its matte finish which accentuates the old fashion feeling of the *Brunch* pattern.

I have found the mercerized cottons to be colorfast and recommend machine-washing the heavier textiles in cool water on a gentle cycle and line drying. The blankets and dishtowels can be machine washed and dried, giving the finished product a soft and luxurious hand. To prevent fading of colors and deterioration of the natural fibers, it is always best to keep all of the textiles out of direct sunlight.

Weft

The rugs, fabrics, and table coverings in this book are woven in a warped-faced technique with the warp mostly covering the weft. Two weft threads, a thick and a thin thread, are used alternately. You will see the weft at the selvage and occasionally peaking out of the body of the weaving, but in this approach the weft has a limited impact on the design. In the throw blankets and curtains, however, I chose a balanced Thick-and-Thin technique instead that allows the weft to show through the warp and thus affects the color of the overall piece. The thick weft yarn for the throws and curtains is a 3/2 mercerized cotton and the thin is a 20/2 mercerized cotton.

The thick weft for the rugs, placemats, and upholstery is a multi-stranded unmercerized cotton available in a variety of colors and sizes depending on its intended purpose.

For the rugs, I recommend rug roping or 2/20 ply, and for the tablerunners I use a 2/8 or 8/16 wound double-stranded. A 4/4 single strand works well for upholstery weight fabrics. Any equivalent size thread or multiple of threads wound together can be used for the weft. Fabric strips cut into various widths can also be used as the thick weft if the unmercerized cotton is unavailable or if the fabric strips are plentiful! A 10/2 cotton yarn is used for the thin weft in the rugs, placemats, and upholstery. I will often use a 16/2 linen thread for my thin weft because it is strong, packs in tightly, and satisfies my desire to keep the tradition of linen in the Rep weave rugs. You'll find the linen to be more expensive, but I think it is worth it.

Weft Recommendations Chart

	THICK	THIN
CURTAINS	3/2	20/2 mercerized
THROW BLANKETS	3/2	20/2 mercerized
DISHTOWELS	4/4 or 3/2	16/2 unmercerized
RUGS	2/20 ply or 8/16 (3 strands)	10/2 unmercerized 16/2 linen
TABLERUNNERS	2/8 ply unmercerized or 8/16 double unmercerized	10/2 mercerized 10/2 mercerized
UPHOLSTERY	4/4 unmercerized	10/2 mercerized

Equipment

Rep weave requires a sturdy loom. The warp threads are so dense that a heavy beat is necessary to pack the threads tightly. A counter-marche loom is helpful because it pulls the warp both up and down, easily separating the dense warp threads. A rug loom will supply the weight and heft you need to tightly pack the rug and a compu-dobby attachment will give you more treadling and designing options. Rep weave can be woven on a simple two-shaft loom, but more shafts will give you greater design capabilities. Depending on the loom size, 15–40 pounds of weight can be added to the beater bar to pack the rug tightly. A boat shuttle is generally used for the thin weft and a ski or rag shuttle works well for the heavy thick weft.

You can weave the lighter weight blanket and curtain fabrics on any loom as they require only a light beat. A double fly-shuttle works well and will make the weaving go more quickly. When using the fly-shuttle, it works best to thread the last two ends at each selvage in a tabby on a separate pair of shafts. This will make the edge threads shift up and down with each weft shot so the weft thread does not pull back into the weaving. We prevent that from happening in the heavier weight weavings by twisting the thick and thin wefts around each other when they are both at the selvage.

Chapter 3:
Techniques and Tips

Setting up the Loom

All weavers have their own preferences for setting up the loom. Fortunately, any basic weaving book can show you how it has been done historically and reliably. Here are some particular tips and techniques I've found helpful when weaving Rep, and you may find them valuable to transfer to other techniques as well.

As you may know, Rep weave is a warp-faced variation of a tabby weave structure. Half of the threads are up and half are down at all times and they completely cover the weft. The weft is alternating thick and thin threads which gives the structure strength and also a wonderful ridge-like texture. One of the things I really like about Rep weave is that it is very consistent and predictable. There are no surprises with this technique; you set up the loom and you know what to expect.

The Beauty of Pairs

Two is a magic number in Rep weave. Two shafts and two treadles are needed for every pattern block. They are worked in pairs as opposites of each other. I always use adjacent shafts as pairs. In other words, 1 & 2 as a pair, 3 & 4 as a pair, and so on. I find it easier to thread the loom when the paired shafts are right next to each other, and treadling is easier as well when the paired treadles are side by side.

Winding & Threading the Warp

For the rugs, runners, placemats, and upholstery, I use a 5/2 pearl cotton for the warp, setting it at 48 epi (ends per inch) with four ends per dent on a 12-dent reed. Rather than threading single threads separately, I recommend threading two ends per heddle to decrease your threading time by half. Plus, you will use half as many heddles. The two threads going through each heddle are wound together to make up one color.

So, when it comes to winding a warp, you can wind four ends at a time by using your fingers to keep each color separate. When you reach the cross, split the four so that two threads go above the warping post and two threads go below, always keeping the two threads of the same

color together. If you are winding a solid color, use four ends of all the same color and split them two and two at the cross. The two threads per color that are wound together stay together when you thread the reed and the heddles. With so many threads to warp, you will find this is a good way to make the process go faster.

To prevent getting an unplanned solid vertical stripe in the finished weaving, it is important to notice which color thread you use first when threading the heddles. Avoid having the same colors next to each other when switching to a new shaft or when changing to a new color on the same shafts. For example, if you are threading yellow and blue threads on shafts 1 & 2, and blue and green threads on shafts 3 & 4, be sure the two blue threads do not end up next to each other. If you forget, which is easy to do, you will see a band of color where you may not want one.

Adjusting for Shrinkage

Rep weave not only eats up heddles, because of all the ends, but is prone to extra shrinkage. In order to compensate for this effect, you need to calculate for it twice. Start with the project length including hems and add an extra 20%. Then add in the loom waste to get your total warp length. While weaving the piece, you will want to add an additional 5–10% beyond your project length to compensate for shrinkage that happens when you remove the piece from the loom. For example, if you are making a 60" rug you will weave the rug to 66" on the loom, not including the hems. This is referred to as the "weave to" length in the project description. I always measure with the loom off tension.

Managing a Dense Warp

One great thing about Rep is that it is easy to keep nice even selvages, even as a beginner. Because of the dense warp, extra warp threads on the edges are unnecessary. The challenge of all those warp ends, however, is the difficulty in winding the warp onto the loom. I always thread the loom front to back, and find it easier to wind on the warp if I remove the lease sticks after threading the loom and before winding on. If you prefer threading back to front, make a cross at both ends of the warp so you can remove the lease sticks before you wind on the warp. You will still have the cross at the end to thread the loom.

My looms all have sectional warping beams which keep the threads stacked up evenly on the back beam. This prevents them from slipping at the edge due to the tight tension required with Rep weave. If you don't have a sectional back beam, here is a trick that will help to keep the warp from shifting. Using sticks that are at least 2–3 inches wider than the warp, place the sticks on the back beam between rounds of warp, about 3–4 per round. Attach a strong cotton string around one end of a stick next to the warp, wind the string across the warp diagonally to the next stick and wrap it around the stick pulling it tight enough to keep the warp in place. Do this every 2–3 rotations as you wind on the warp and you shouldn't have any trouble with the warp slipping at the edges on the back beam.

A stiff kitchen brush comes in handy if the threads get snarly after winding on the loom, which they usually do. I untangle the warp by brushing the threads smooth into 1½" bundles. Then I tie them off with an overhand knot. I continue by lashing the warp bundles onto the front beam and adjust the lash cord for even tension across the width of the warp.

Rep Weaving Tips

The tension on the loom should be very tight when weaving the heavy rugs and fabrics. This allows the threads to compact together with a hard swing or two on the beater. The harder you beat, the stronger and more durable the finished textile will be, so don't be afraid to whack it hard. Because the Rep weave warp is so dense, it is easy to keep the edges even when weaving. A temple is not necessary and the weft can be laid in straight without an arch for take up. While weaving the rugs and table runners, I recommend twisting the thick weft at the corner to make the weft loop small and consistent along the edges.

When starting a new thick thread, unwind about 4" of the old and the new thread. Lay half the new thread over half the old with the tail ends lying on the surface of the weaving. Once you have the ends secured with a weft shot, you can cut them off close to the weaving surface for a smooth finish. This eliminates a double thickness or bump in the woven textile. It is best to add the new thread away from the edge to keep the short end from pulling out of the rug with use.

Thick-and-Thin Technique & Tips

Years ago a fellow weaver told me about a great production loom for sale and asked me if I was interested. I bought it not sure what I would do with it since I couldn't weave Rep on it. Six months later, I saw a blanket woven in a Thick-and-Thin technique which was just the missing link for me to connect my Rep weave designs to this luxurious blanket weight. Now I love weaving this lighter weight fabric.

The blanket and curtain weight textiles are lighter, and the warp is opened up to 20 ends per inch, still using a 5/2 pearl cotton. The warp is threaded differently from Rep with only two ends per dent on a 10 dent reed and one end through each heddle. You will still use two threads to make up one color, but the color pair will split up when threading the heddles.

If you find a knot in a warp thread when winding the warp, I recommend adding two feet of extra warp to that thread and tying it into a slip knot so that the knot can be removed later while weaving. Place the extra thread and the slip knot between the warp knot and the cross on the warping reel. The extra thread can be untied when you are weaving, and the knot can be moved forward or back to be placed out of the weaving area. Or, the knot can be cut out and the two ends laid in with the next thick weft shot. Instead of splicing, simply overlap the weft ends for this join or when you need to add more thread.

The beat for the blankets and other light weight fabrics is very gentle. Just a tap will push the weft down and next to the last shot. After hemming, you will want to machine wash and dry the blanket to full the fabric and bring out the beautiful softness of the cotton.

Depending on the pattern, the selvage warp thread will not catch with every weft pass, and this could cause the weft to slip back into the weaving on the next pattern shot. To prevent this from happening, you will want to always twist the thick and thin weft threads around each other when they are both at the same edge and before you send the next shot through the shed. In this photograph, the thin weft is going over the last warp thread so it will need to pass under the thick weft before it goes into the shed. If the thin weft were under the last warp thread, then it would pass over the thick weft before going into the shed.

I used to find it very annoying when I would go to hem a piece and the weft threads had started to pull out. An easy solution I discovered is to place a narrow bead of non-toxic clear glue over the last weft thread before you cut the warp off the loom. You can even thin the glue with a little water and keep it for just this purpose. By creating a standard double fold hem you will hide any evidence of the glue.

Chapter 4: **Projects**

The 18 projects featured here are functional textiles for the home; including, rugs, runners, upholstery and pillow fabrics, towels, curtains, throws, and bed coverings. The rugs also work beautifully on the wall as art pieces. I love both the versatility and utility of woven creations possible with Rep weave.

By simply changing the weft size, the same warp can be used for a heavy rug, medium weight table runner, and finer weight upholstery fabric. By opening up the warp to a balanced Thick-and-Thin weave and using a much lighter beat, the same designs can be used to make soft and fluid fabrics desirable for towels, curtains, throws, and bed coverings. The upholstered pieces are recycled furniture found in local Good Will stores and antique shops with the exception of the brown sofa which was a collaboration with a furniture maker. Apply the ideas and patterns in these projects to fulfill a need in your home, to create a gift, or simply to inspire your own weaving process.

Bedroom Rugs & Pillows

The *Oleana* pattern is a traditional design usually woven in two colors (pattern #1), but in this version (pattern #2) I added multiple colors and eliminated parts of the design so that the circle motif is prominent and looks contemporary in keeping with the spread. The smaller pattern scale and deeper color tones are intentionally chosen to contrast with the large pattern blocks and lighter colors in the spread. The irregular repeats of the circles and the stripes complement the contemporary style. All three of these designs, and more, can be woven from the same warp set up. Have fun exploring different treadling sequences.

Pattern 1

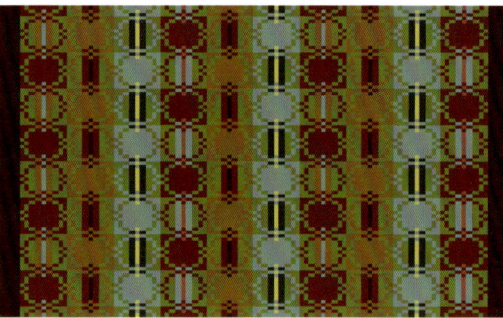
Pattern 2

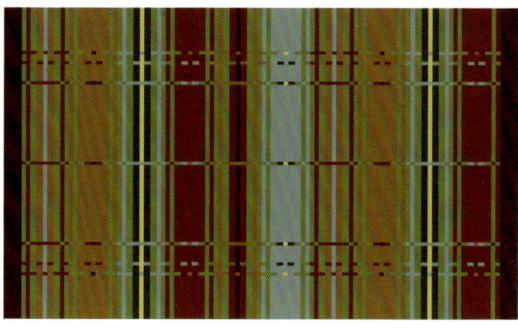
Stripe

DESIGN *Oleana*

TECHNIQUE Warp-faced Rep weave, 8 shafts and 8 treadles

FINISHED SIZE Rug patterns 1 & 2 – 20" x 42", stripe 20" x 6', fabric 55"

MATERIALS See color chart in back for exact project color quantities.

WARP 5/2 pearl cotton – length: 6' rug and 55" pillow fabric, 17' warp.

WEFT Rug: thick 480 yards, 8/16MB unmercerized cotton black triple stranded. Fabric: thick 200 yards, 8/8MB or 4/4 unmercerized cotton black. Both thin 10/2 pearl cotton, 410 yards black.

REED 12-dent reed, 4 ends per dent, 2 ends per heddle

SETT 48 ends per inch

WIDTH IN REED 20"

WEFT SETT Rug 18 rows (thick and thin) =5". Fabric 30 rows (thick and thin) = 5"

NUMBER OF ENDS 960

- **A** U77 Dusty Coral / U128 Quince
- **B** U149 Burnt Orange / U32 Lipstick
- **C** W5604 Willow / U87 Verdant
- **D** U49 Larch Green / U87 Verdant
- **E** U95 Mineral / U94 Tyrol
- **F** U46 Champagne / U7 Oak
- **G** U122 Mead / U145 Bark
- **H** U25 Medium Brown / U145 Bark

Warp Sequence

	1	2	3	4	5	6	7	8	9	10	11	12	13	14	15	16	17	18	19	20	21
A			4																		
B		14	6	4	6	14				6		6			14	6	4	6	14		6
C		14			14	14			14	14			14	14			14	14		14	14
D				6		6									6		6				
E		6		6		14	6	4	6	14						4		14	6	4	6	14
F					4											4					
G									14	6	4	6	14		6		6				14	6
H	40									4											

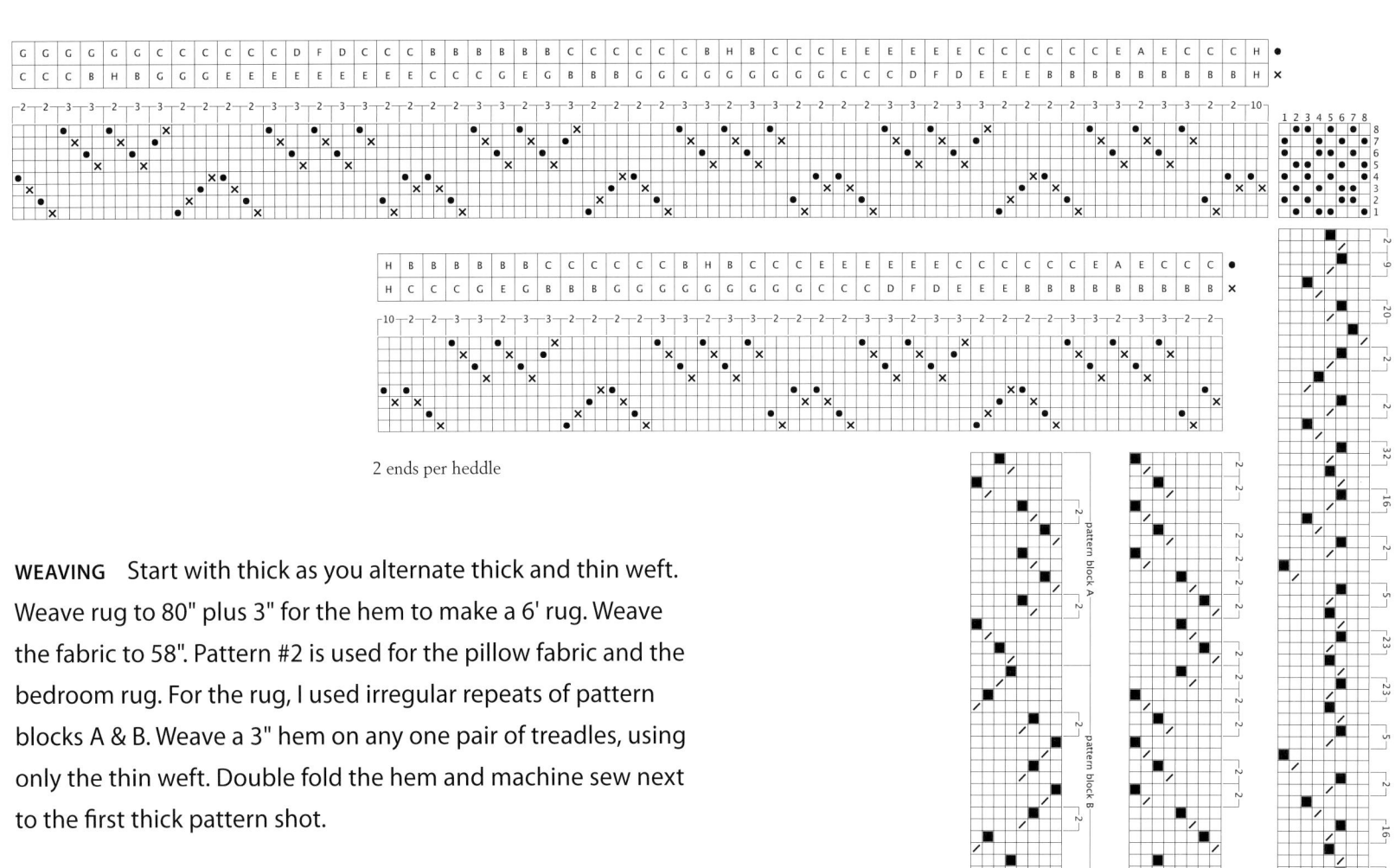

2 ends per heddle

WEAVING   Start with thick as you alternate thick and thin weft. Weave rug to 80" plus 3" for the hem to make a 6' rug. Weave the fabric to 58". Pattern #2 is used for the pillow fabric and the bedroom rug. For the rug, I used irregular repeats of pattern blocks A & B. Weave a 3" hem on any one pair of treadles, using only the thin weft. Double fold the hem and machine sew next to the first thick pattern shot.

Bedroom Table Runner

The original built-in dresser dividing the bedroom and the kitchen is the perfect place to showcase this lovely runner. Its playful pattern integrates colors from the surrounding rooms. Beware that this seemingly simple block pattern uses 10 shafts and 10 treadles to create the shifting of blocks and color that add complexity and depth.

Warp Sequence

A		12								12		12		12		12		12				72
B	12	12		12							12	12		12	12		12		12	12		120
C				12	12												12			12		48
D			12				12										12		12			36
E		12																12		12		36
F										12												12
G												12										12
H							12		12		12											36
I				12			12		12	12				12								60
J		12		12		12		12														36
K	12			12	12	12	12	12	12													84
L			12	12	12	12	12	12														72
																						624

- **A** U53 Scarab / S42 Hemp
- **B** S103 Tunisian Teal / U134 Cactus
- **C** U98 Mountain
- **D** U146 Periwinkle / U119 Hummingbird
- **E** U119 Hummingbird / U126 Denim
- **F** W2574 Heather
- **G** U46 Champagne / U140 Safari
- **H** S326 Antelope
- **I** S109 Khaki / U108 Light Rust
- **J** U149 Burnt Orange
- **K** U149 Burnt Orange / S91 Tobacco
- **L** S143 Burgundy / U122 Mead

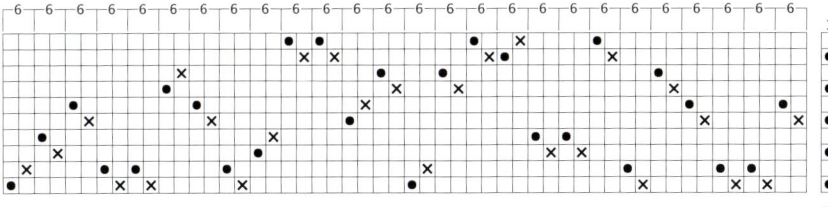

2 ends per heddle

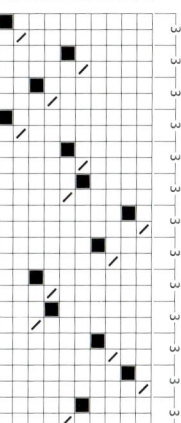

DESIGN *Waterdance*

TECHNIQUE Warp-faced Rep weave, 10 shafts and 10 treadles

FINISHED SIZE 13" x 60"

MATERIALS See color chart in back for exact project color quantities.

WARP 5/2 pearl cotton, 10' warp

WEFT Thick 140 yards, 8/16MB unmercerized cotton #8266 green or black, thin 167yards, 10/2 pearl cotton, black

REED 12-dent reed, 4 ends per dent, 2 ends per heddle

SETT 48 epi

WIDTH IN REED 13"

WEFT SETT 48 rows (thick and thin) = 8"

NUMBER OF ENDS 624

WEAVING Start with thick as you alternate thick and thin weft. Weave the runner to 64" plus 2½" each hem. Weave the hem on any one pair of treadles, using only the thin weft. Double fold the hem and machine sew next to the first thick pattern shot.

Kitchen Rugs

The kitchen rugs shift in color from the bedroom. The blues go to turquoise, the greens more olive, reds more orange into salmon with the addition of dark maroon and dusty purple. Some of the colors are the same, tying the rooms together. The short rug is the full width of the pattern and the long rug needed to be narrower to fit in the space, so I just reduced the warp width from one side and the salmon color became the center. With the variation in the long runner design, the pattern still looks great. The rugs coordinate, yet each makes a strong statement of its own. The long runner covers the trap door to the basement. A house with a trap door, how fun! The little stool is actually a plant holder for which I made an upholstered top. Now I can store things in it and sit on it, too.

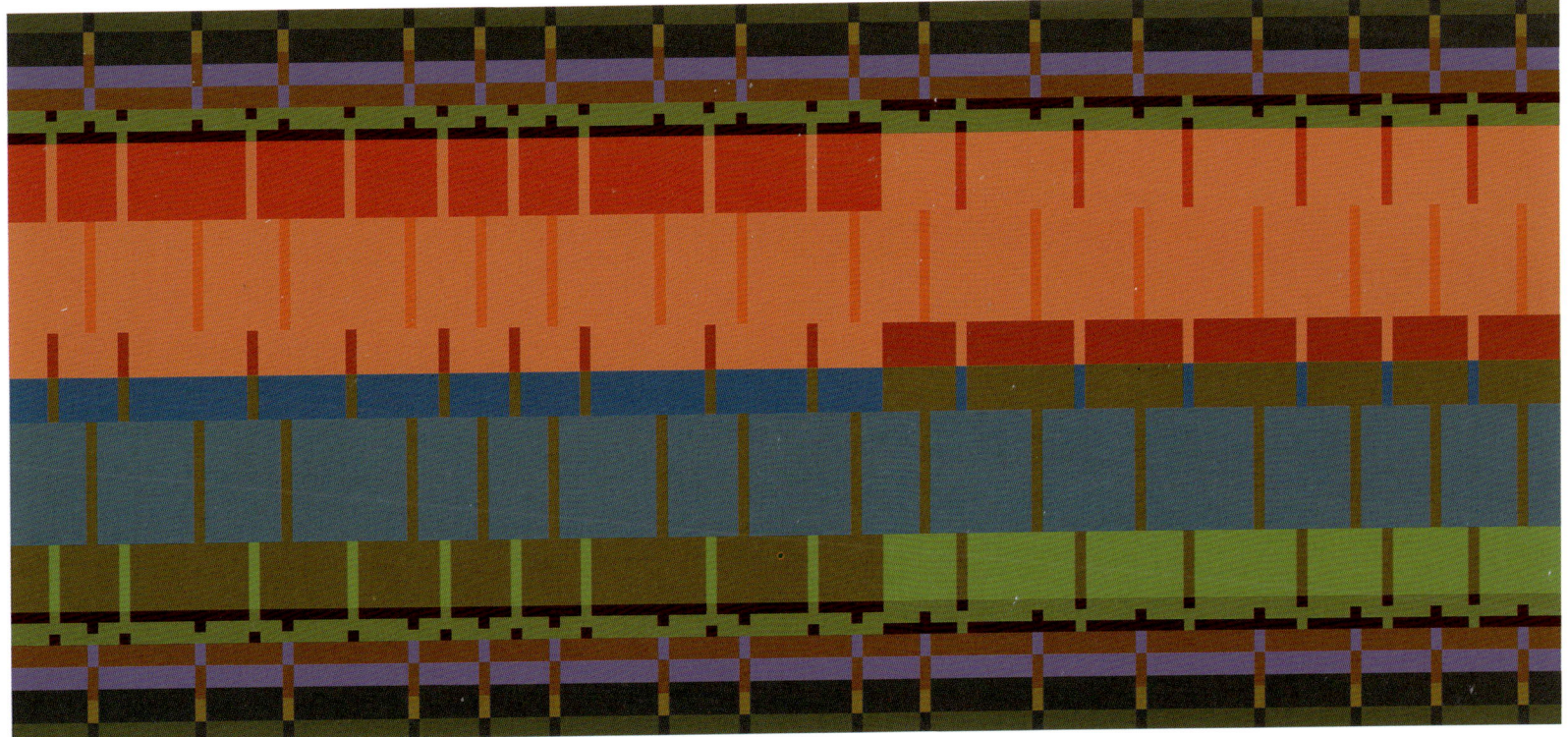

Long *Pinwheel* rug, full width

DESIGN *Pinwheel*

TECHNIQUE Warp-faced Rep weave, 8 shafts and 6 treadles

FINISHED SIZE Short rug 44 x 50", long rug 30" x 86", upholstery 22"

MATERIALS See color chart in back for exact project color quantities.

WARP 5/2 pearl cotton–20' warp

WEFT Rug: thick 308 yards, 8/16MB unmercerized cotton #8266 green triple stranded. Fabric: thick 161 yards, 8/8MB or 4/4 unmercerized cotton black. Thin 10/2 pearl cotton 650 yards dark green or black.

REED 12-dent reed, 4 ends per dent, 2 ends per heddle

SETT 48 ends per inch

WIDTH IN REED 44" short rug and fabric, 30" long rug

WEFT SETT Rug: 18 rows (thick and thin) = 5". Fabric: 30 rows (thick and thin) = 5".

NUMBER OF ENDS 2112

WEAVING Start with thick as you alternate thick and thin weft. Weave the short rug to 56" in length plus 3" each hem. Weave the long rug to 93" plus 3" each hem. Weave the fabric to 24". The fabric can be used for upholstery or for pillow coverings. Weave the hem on any one pair of treadles, using only the thin weft. Double fold the hem and machine sew next to the first thick pattern shot.

- A U77 Dusty Coral / U108 Light Rust
- B W7198 Burnt Sienna / U108 Light Rust
- C S91 Tobacco / U108 Light Rust
- D U149 Burnt Orange / S77 Brick
- E U34 Maroon
- F U119 Hummingbird
- G U122 Mead / U145 Bark
- H U87 Verdant / U106 Persian Green
- I U87 Verdant
- J U50 Avocado
- K S103 Tunisian Teal / U103 Peacock
- L U48 Dark Turk / U98 Mountain Green
- M U98 Mountain Green / U49 Larch Green
- N U49 Larch Green / S109 Khaki
- O U62 Moss Green / U122 Mead

Warp Sequence

	1	2	3	4	5	6	7	8	9	10	11	12	13	Total
A					96	176	64							336
B						176								176
C							64							64
D					96									96
E				48						48				96
F			64								64			128
G		16	64								64	16		160
H				48						48				96
I								64	160	112				336
J									112					112
K									160					160
L								64						64
M	32	32	16								16	32	32	160
N	32												32	64
O		32										32		64
														2112

Pinwheel fabric

Pinwheel rug

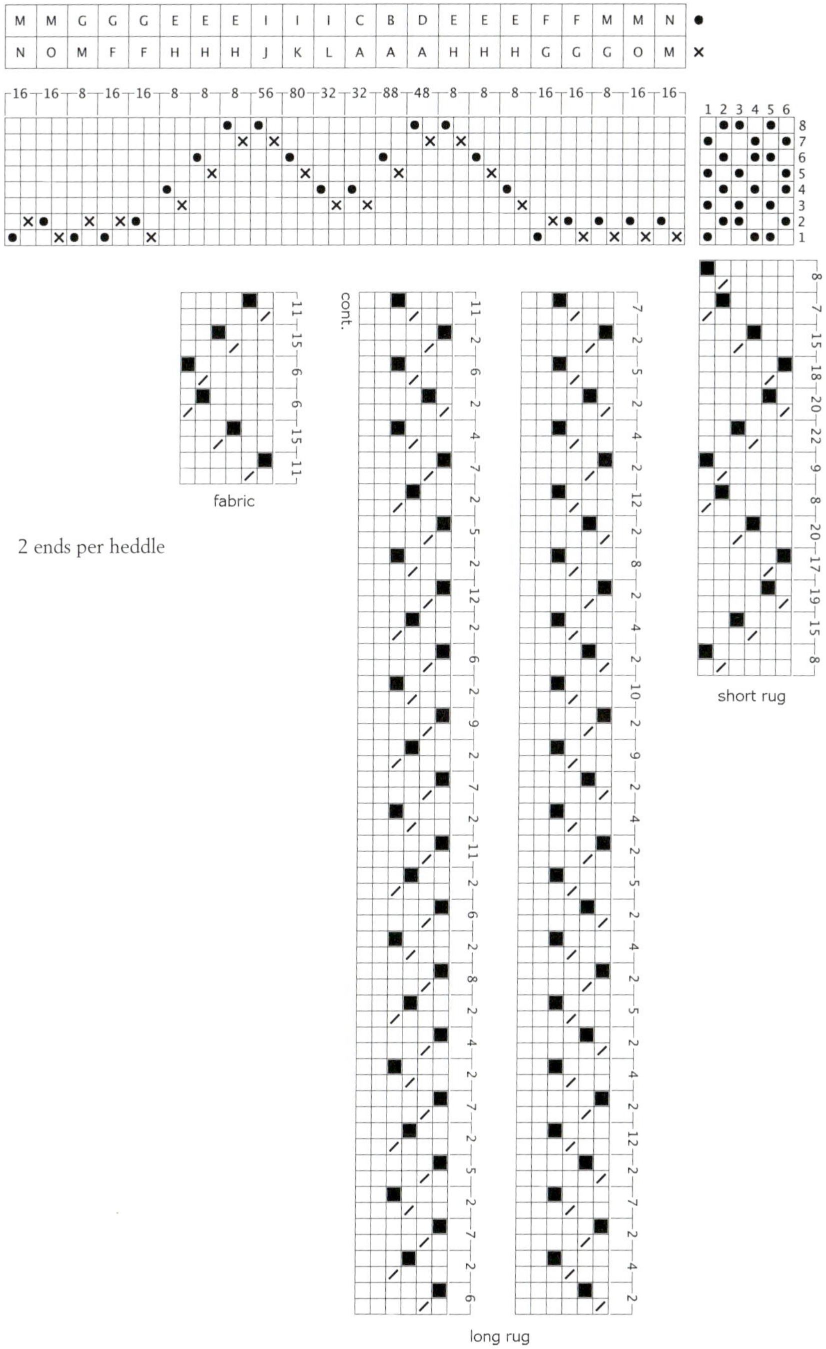

2 ends per heddle

fabric

short rug

long rug

Dishtowels

The dishtowel brings us back to an earlier time with this traditional Scandinavian pattern. Even the muted colors reflect a vintage style. Yet the colors and mood of this design work well with the other colors in the house by pulling in the bright orange red, turquoise blue, and yellow green in the rugs next to it.

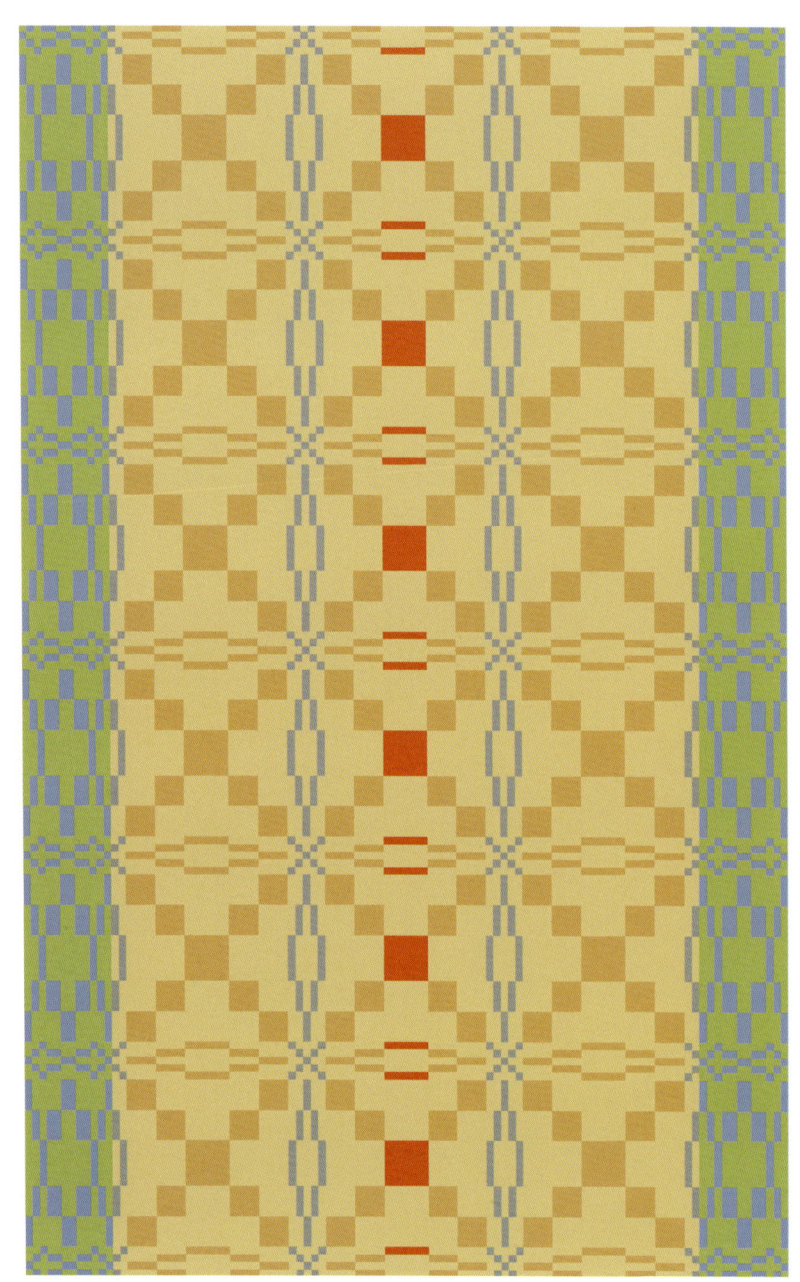

DESIGN *Brunch*

TECHNIQUE   Balanced Thick-and-Thin, 6 shafts and 6 treadles

FINISHED SIZE   3 towels, each towel 16" x 28" after washing

MATERIALS   See color chart in back for exact project color quantities.

WARP   8/2 unmercerized cotton–13' warp

WEFT   Thick 3/2 pearl cotton, S712 Beechnut 443 yards. Thin 20/2 pearl cotton, U43 Beige 578 yards.

REED   12-dent reed , 2 ends per dent, 1 end per heddle

SETT   24 ends per inch

WIDTH IN REED   17.83"

WEFT SETT   41 rows (thick and thin) = 5"

NUMBER OF ENDS   428

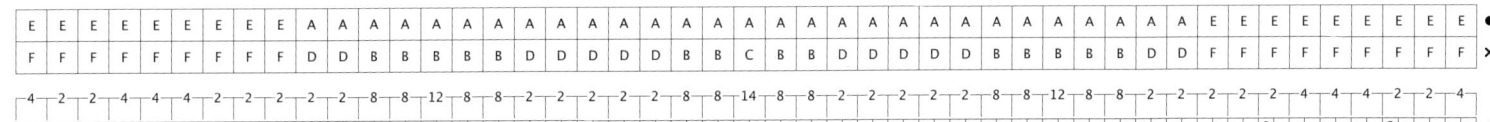
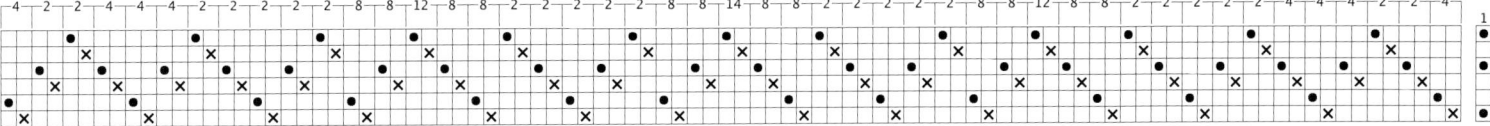

Single ends threaded through the heddles

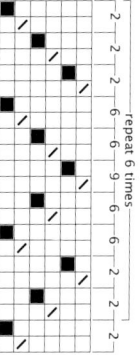

WEAVING Start with thick as you alternate thick and thin weft. Weave to 36" plus 2½" each hem. Note the beat is much lighter on the dishtowel weight than when weaving a rug. Weave the hem on any one pair of treadles, using only the thin weft. Double fold the hem and machine sew next to the first thick pattern shot. After hemming, machine wash warm and dry to finish the towels. Substituting an unmercerized weft of comparable weight will make the towel more absorbent.

- **A** MB5069 Chamois / MB1451 Ivoire
- **B** MB5212 Honey / MB1183 Cannelle
- **C** MB5213 Cayenne
- **D** MB8115 Stone
- **E** MB1934 Vert Nil / MB4269 Limette Pale
- **F** MB112 Slate / MB94 Vieux Bleu

Warp Sequence

A		4	44	10	16	14	16	10	44	4	162
B			44		16		16		44		120
C						14					14
D		4		10				10		4	28
E	26										26	52
F	26										26	52
											428

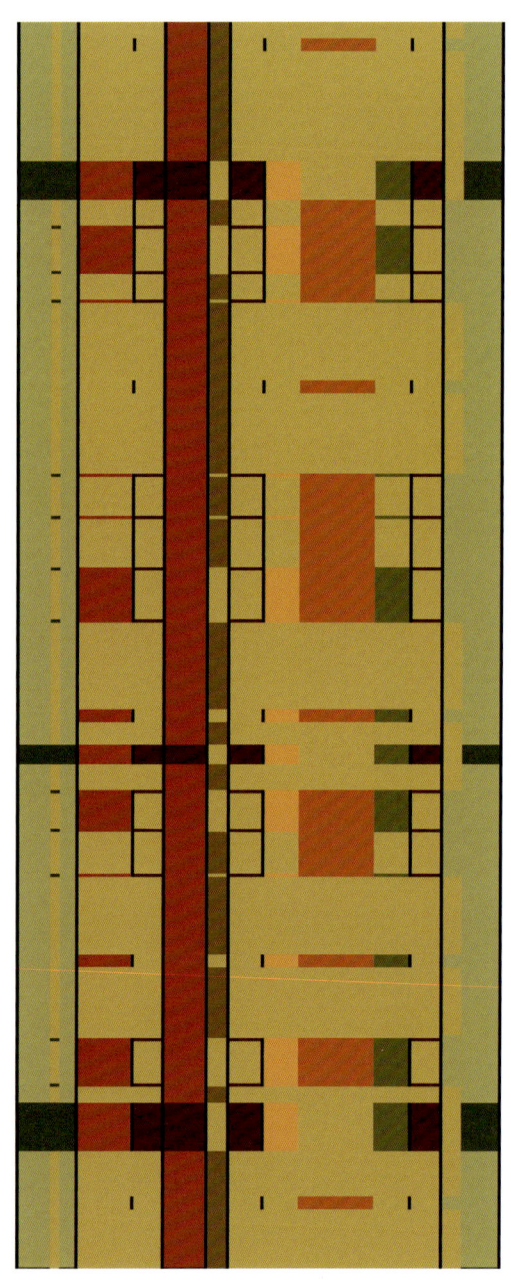

DESIGN *Beyond*

TECHNIQUE   Warp-faced Rep weave, 10 shafts and 10 treadles

If you only have 8 shafts, change shafts 9 & 10 to a solid black line and thread those ends on any shaft pair.

FINISHED SIZE   Rug: 29" x 58", fabric for upholstery or pillows: depending on desired size

MATERIALS   See color chart in back for exact project color quantities. Colors calculated for rug only, 10' warp add more for fabric or tote (pg. 72)

WARP   5/2 pearl cotton, same warp for rug and fabric

WEFT   Rug: thick rug weight 189 yards, 8/16MB unmercerized cotton black triple stranded, thin 10/2 pearl cotton 260 yards black.
Fabric: thick 8/8MB or 4/4 unmercerized cotton, thin 10/2 pearl cotton black, 174 yards each per yard of finished fabric.

REED   12-dent reed, 4 ends per dent, 2 ends per heddle

SETT   48 ends per inch

WIDTH IN REED   29"

WEFT SETT   Rug 18 rows (thick and thin) = 5". Fabric 30 rows (thick and thin) = 5".

NUMBER OF ENDS   1392

WEAVING   Start with thick as you alternate thick and thin weft. Weave rug to 65" plus 3" each hem. Weave the hem on any one pair of treadles, using only the thin weft. Double fold the hem and machine sew next to the first thick pattern shot. This particular chair required 16' of fabric, a dark brown soft leather was used on the foot rest. The fabric can be used for upholstery, pillow coverings, and tote bag.

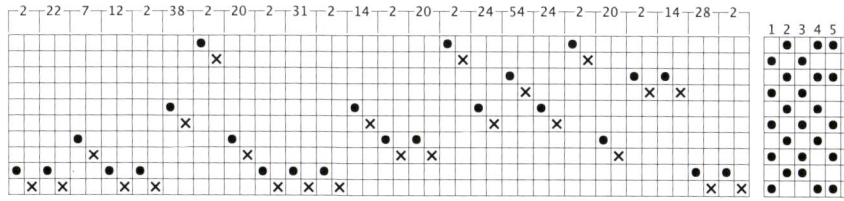

2 ends per heddle

Warp Sequence

A	56														24	14	44		138
B			48																48
C										62		76							138
D				108															108
E					48														48
F								28											28
G	56	28													24		44		152
H		28		40	4	48	108	48	4	40	28		40	4	76		14		482
I			40	4			40			62	40			4					182
J	8		8	4		4	8		8		8	4	8					8	68
																			1392

- **A** S38 Dill / U49 Larch
- **B** S38 Dill / U106 Persian Green
- **C** S77 Brick / U99 Dark Sierra
- **D** U108 Light Rust / W7129 Golden Ocher
- **E** U46 Champagne / U7 Oak
- **F** U87 Verdant / S109 Khaki
- **G** S38 Dill / S42 Hemp
- **H** U43 Beige
- **I** U25 Medium Brown
- **J** S2 Black

Self-closing Tote Bag

I have been making tote bags for years and was always stumped with what kind of closure to use because snaps, buttons, and zippers all seemed so inconvenient. I got this slip-through closure idea from a felted bag I saw that has a short handle and a long handle that slips through the shorter one. I took it a step further and attached the short handle to the bag so the bag stays shut when you carry it by the long handle that goes over the shoulder. It is easy to open and close with a generous opening to get notebooks and bigger items into the bag. The tote is made of fabric from the living room *Beyond* design, so follow the directions for loom set-up as per the rug.

1. WEAVE the desired fabric pattern to 29" x 42". Cut the body piece 21" x 42". Cut 2 handles 3½" x 42" and 3½" x 21".

DIAGRAM A

2. HANDLES Zig-zag along one long side and the two short ends of both handles. Fold each one lengthwise into thirds leaving the zig-zagged edge on the top (handle is 1¼" wide). Sew (straight stitch) down the center of the handle.

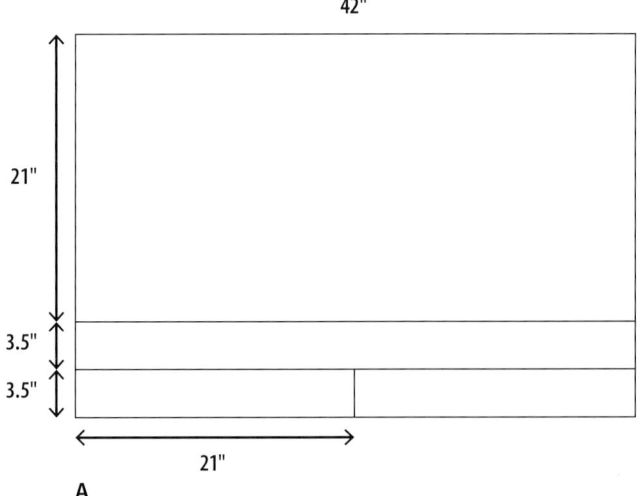

A

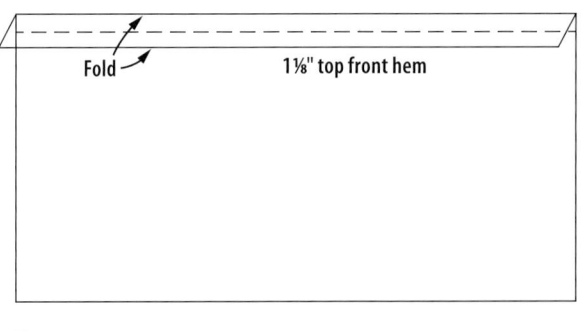

B

3. BODY OF BAG Double fold top edge of bag to front side and sew in place to make a 1⅛" hem. **DIAGRAM B**

Center seam: Fold fabric into cylinder with right side out overlapping edges 1½". Turn top edge under ½" and sew close to the fold leaving 1" of fabric on inside edge from the seam. To hide the raw edge, turn the fabric inside-out, fold the 1" flap under ½" and sew next to the fold. **DIAGRAM C**

4. BOTTOM SEAM With the right side out, fold the bag in half with seam down the center. Sew ⅜" from the bottom edge. Turn the bag inside-out and sew ½" from bottom edge enclosing the raw edge.

5. BOTTOM GUSSET With the bag inside-out, fold the corner open into a triangle and pin flat. Sew 5½" across the corner 3" down from the point. **DIAGRAM D**

Fold the corner at this stitch line and firmly tack the point to the bottom of the bag.

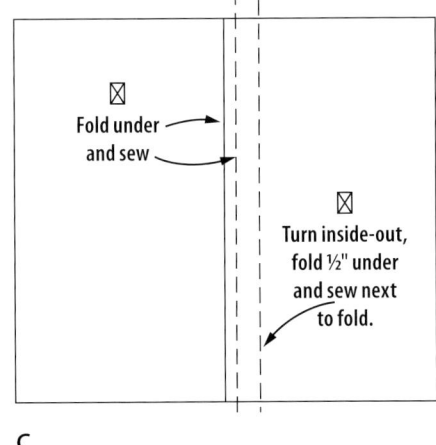

C

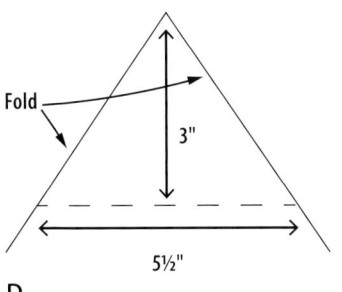

D

6. LONG HANDLE With the bag inside-out, pin one end of the long handle with seam showing 5" from side of bag and 6" down from top edge. Twist the handle 6 times and pin the other end. Sew both ends securely to the bag.
DIAGRAMS E & F

* If you don't want the slip-through closure, make both handles long and attach them as described here.

** A pocket can be sewn in between the handles if desired; a lighter weight twill fabric works well.

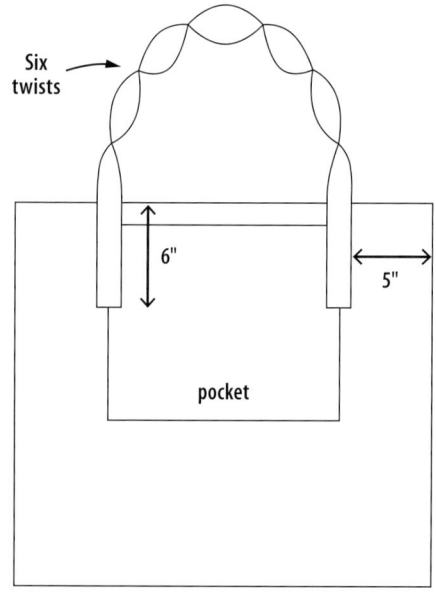

E

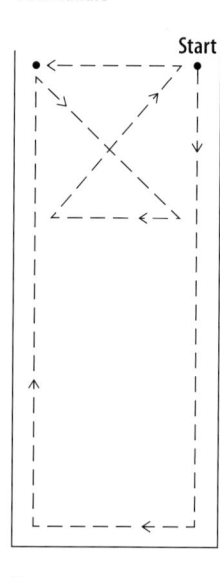

F

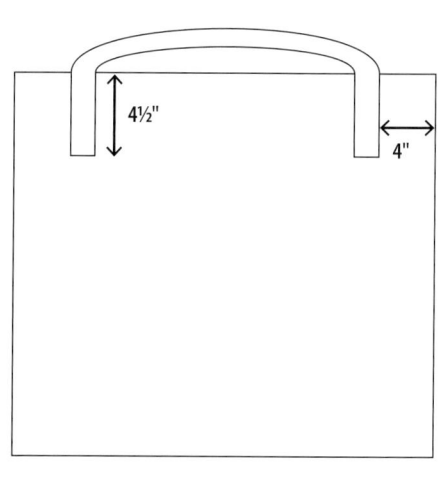

G

7. SHORT HANDLE With the bag inside-out, pin one end of the short handle, with seam showing, 4" from side of bag, 4½" down from top edge. Do not twist short handle. Leave a small arch in the handle and pin the other end before sewing both ends in place. **DIAGRAM G**

Turn bag right side out, put long handle through short handle and sew short handle to the top inside edge of bag between the ends on the short-handle side. Leave a 2" opening around each side of the long handle so that it can slide easily to open and close the bag. **DIAGRAM H**

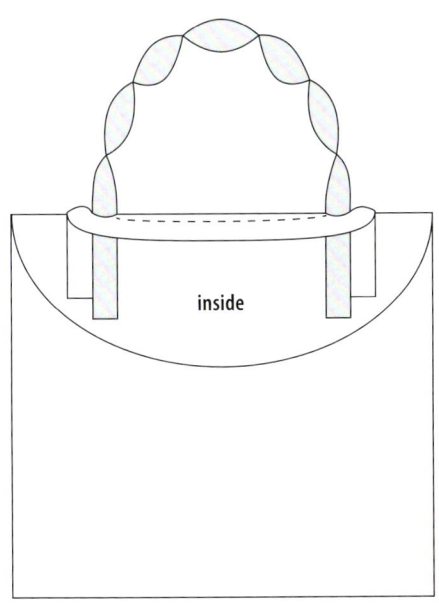

H

Dining Room Table Runner & Placemats

Greens were chosen as the emphasis in this area to reflect the garden outside the dining room window. This fun irregular pattern, reduced from the rug size in the bathroom, works well in the smaller scale. I also use fewer colors for this smaller size focusing on green and rust with a dash of yellow and black from the kitchen rugs.

DESIGN *Conservatory*

TECHNIQUE   Warp-faced Rep weave, 6 shafts and 8 treadles

FINISHED SIZE   Table runner 13" x 40", 6 placemats 13" x 18" each

MATERIALS   See color chart in back for exact project color quantities.

WARP   5/2 pearl cotton for the table runner and 6 placemats, 19' warp

WEFT   Thick 338 yards, 8/16 unmercerized cotton black. Thin 367 yards, 10/2 pearl cotton black.

REED   12-dent reed, 4 ends per dent, 2 ends per heddle

SETT   48 ends per inch

WIDTH IN REED   13"

WEFT SETT   48 rows (thick and thin) = 8"

NUMBER OF ENDS   624

Placemat

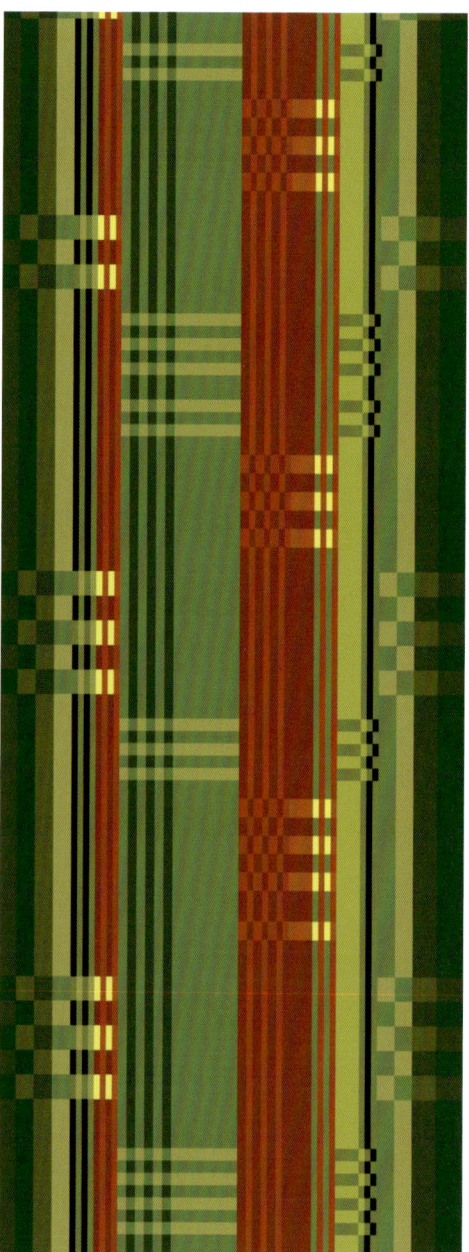

Table Runner

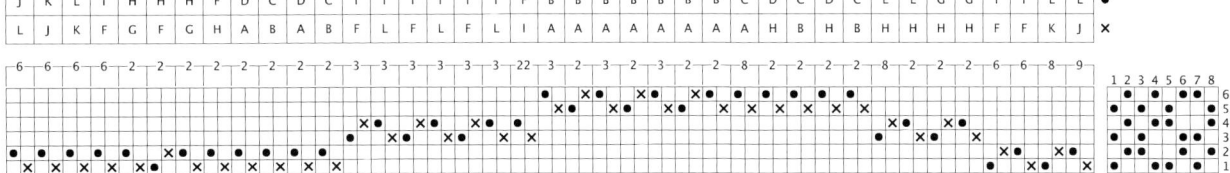

2 ends per heddle

WEAVING Start with thick as you alternate thick and thin weft. Weave the runner to 42" plus 2½" each hem. Weave each placemat to 19". Start and end each placemat with ½" of warp for fringe and weave 3 rows of thin weft. To finish, machine sew along the last thin weft. To finish the runner, double fold the hem and machine sew next to the first thick pattern shot.

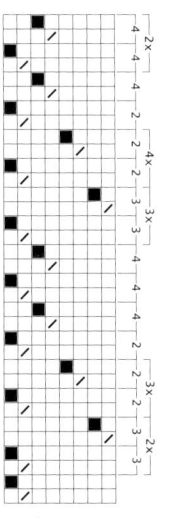

placemats

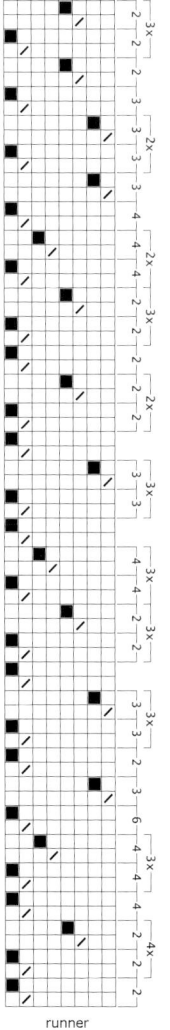

runner

- **A** S768 Clay / U122 Mead
- **B** U77 Dusty Coral / U108 Light Rust
- **C** U108 Light Rust / U61 Topaz
- **D** U139 Chamois
- **E** U84 Gold Dust / U140 Safari
- **F** U84 Gold Dust / S42 Hemp
- **G** S2 Black
- **H** S38 Dill / S42 Hemp
- **I** U134 Cactus / U87 Verdant
- **J** U8 Evergreen / U49 Larch Green
- **K** S109 Khaki / U49 Larch Green
- **L** U49 Larch Green

A						16	34					4		4						58
B			4		4		34					4		4						50
C			4		4	16						4		4						32
D				4		4						4		4						16
E			20																	20
F		24					44		6		6		6			4		4	12		106
G			8												4		4			16
H			8	20	4		4							4	4	4	4			52
I		24					44	6	6	6	6	6						12		116
J	18																	12	12	42
K		16														12	12			40
L	18	16						6		6		6						12	12	76
																				624

Warp Sequence

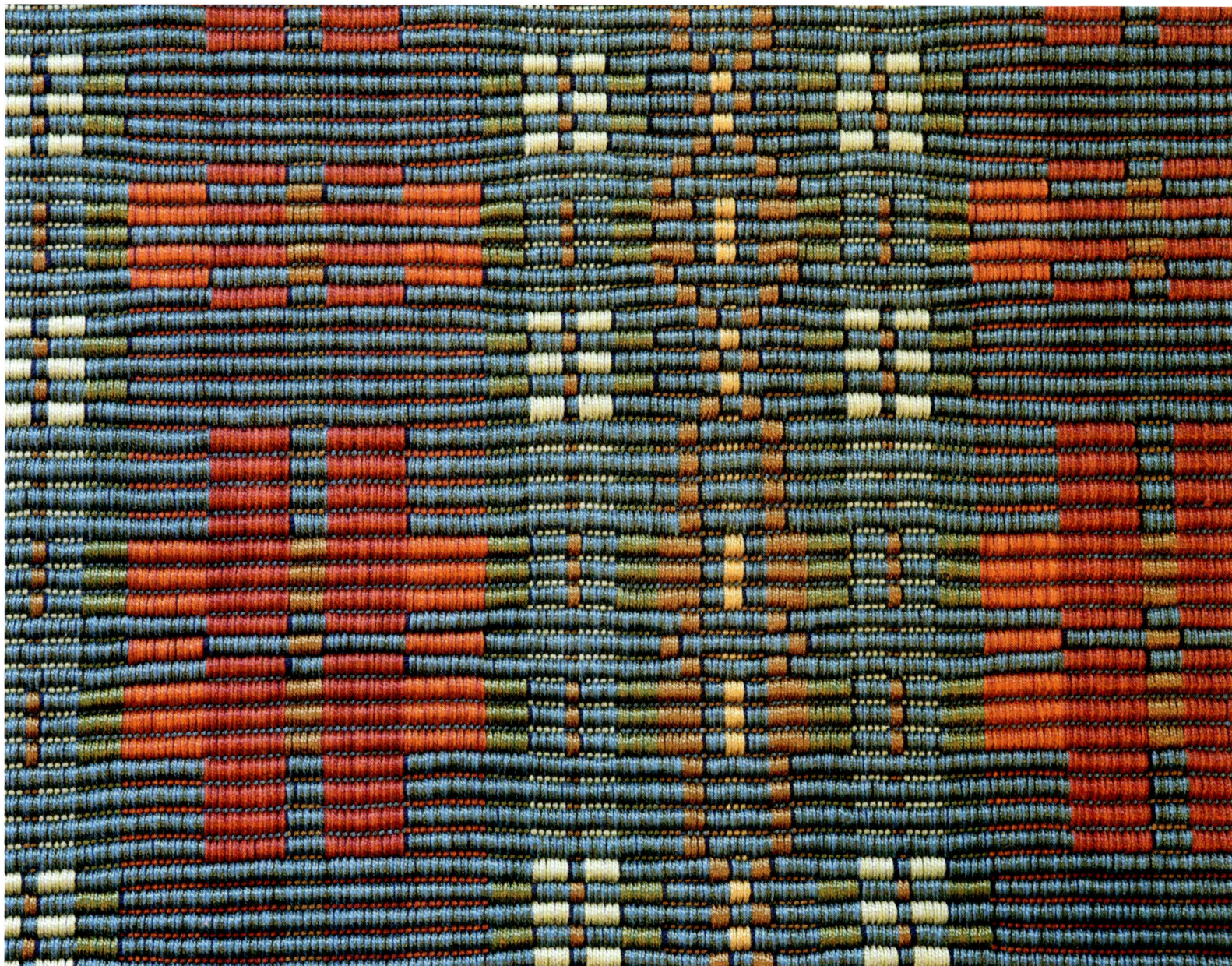

DESIGN *Patchwork*

TECHNIQUE Warp-faced Rep weave, 8 shafts and 10 treadles. If you only have 8 treadles, you can retie the tie-up for treadles 9 & 10 onto treadles 1 and 2 for the top and bottom blue border. Or, you can just eliminate the blue border.

FINISHED SIZE 5' x 4'

MATERIALS See color chart in back for exact project color quantities.

WARP 5/2 pearl cotton, 9' warp

WEFT Thick 285 yards, 8/16MB unmercerized cotton black triple stranded. Thin 432 yards 10/2 pearl cotton black.

REED 12-dent reed, 4 ends per dent, 2 ends per heddle

SETT 48 ends per inch

WIDTH IN REED 60"

WEFT SETT 17 rows (thick and thin) = 5"

NUMBER OF ENDS 2884

Warp Sequence

								5x							
A	96	14	12	10	4	10	12	18	6	18	12	10	4	10	12	22
B					4			18		18			4			
C									6							
D				10		10						10		10		
E			12				12				12				12	
F		14														
G																22

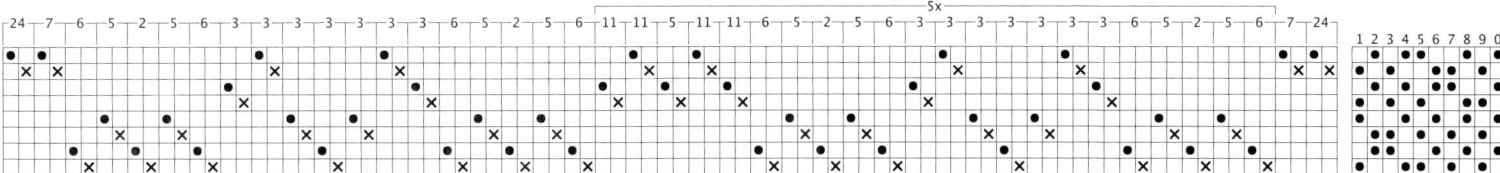

2 ends per heddle

WEAVING Start with thick as you alternate thick and thin weft. Weave the rug to 53" plus 3" each hem. Weave the hem on any one pair of treadles, using only the thin weft. Double fold the hem and machine sew next to the first thick pattern shot.

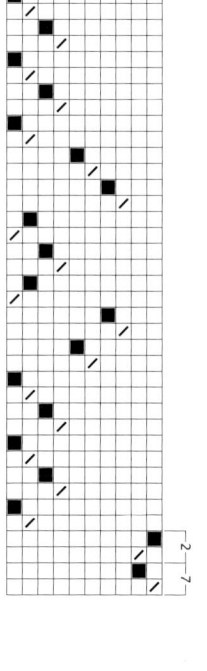
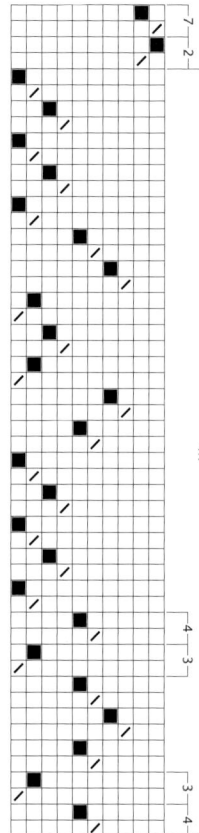

22	22	12	10	4	10	12	18	6	18	12	10	4	10	12	14	96	1538
				4			18		18			4					314
								6									36
			10		10						10		10				240
		12				12				12				12			288
22															14		248
	22																220
																	2884

A U103 Peacock / U98 Mountain Green
B U122 Mead
C U29 Old Gold / W7453 Amber Gold
D W5604 Willow Green
E U87 Verdant / U62 Moss Green
F S77 Brick / U24 Garnet
G S77 Brick / U149 Burnt Orange

Garden Sofa Upholstery & Rug

This project began with a wonderful old wicker sofa discovered at a rummage sale. It had seen better days. The fabric was torn and the back was pushed out. I immediately envisioned it reconditioned handsomely with new upholstery and pillows. This ensemble illustrates how you can play with scale to create varied effects. The new seat cushion fabric is a small scale pattern with lots of color that gives almost a stripe effect to the upholstery. The pillows incorporate the same pattern using a few of the same colors in a larger size that shows off the pattern motifs for a nice contrast with the seat cushions. The same gray-green background color enhances the compatibility of the cushions and the pillows.

DESIGN *Patchwork*

TECHNIQUE Warp-faced Rep weave, 8 shafts and 10 treadles. If you only have 8 treadles, you can retie the tie-up for treadles 9 & 10 onto treadles 1 and 2 for the top and bottom green border. Or, you can just eliminate the border.

FINISHED SIZE 42" x 36" rug
36" fabric for pillows or upholstery, 11' warp

MATERIALS See color chart in back for exact project color quantities.

WARP 5/2 pearl cotton, rug and fabric, 11' warp

WEFT Rug: Thick 160 yards, 8/16MB unmercerized cotton black triple stranded. Thin 265 yards 10/2 pearl cotton black.
Fabric: Thick 266 yards 8/8MB unmercerized cotton or 4/4 cotton black. Thin 266 yards 10/2 pearl cotton black.

REED 12-dent reed, 4 ends per dent, 2 ends per heddle

SETT 48 ends per inch

WIDTH IN REED 42"

WEFT SETT Rug: 17 rows (thick and thin) = 5",
Fabric: 30 rows (thick and thin) = 5"

NUMBER OF ENDS 2016

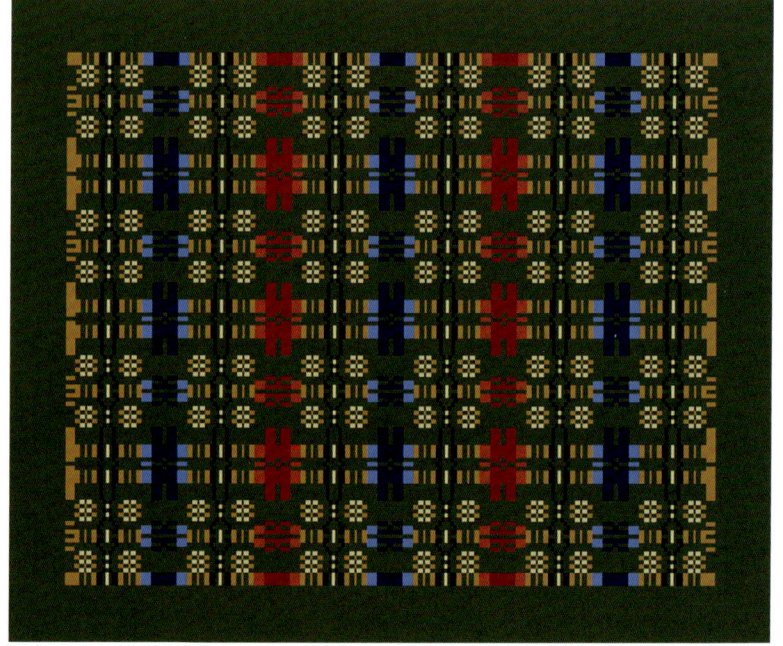

Rug

WEAVING The threading draft depicts the pattern from the beginning to the center. You will need to reverse the threading order from the center continuing to the other edge while maintaining odd/even alternations of shafts. Whether weaving a rug or fabric, start with thick as you alternate thick and thin weft. Weave the top and bottom border to the same size as the solid green side borders.

For the 36" rug, you will use 3 pattern repeats and weave to 40" plus 3" each hem. For the fabric, weave to 38", no hem, border optional.

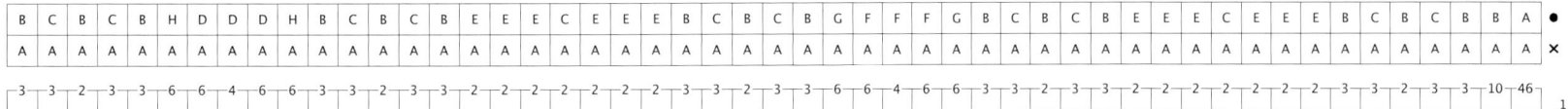

2 ends per heddle
Repeat threading units from center back to edge while maintaining odd-even alternation of shafts.

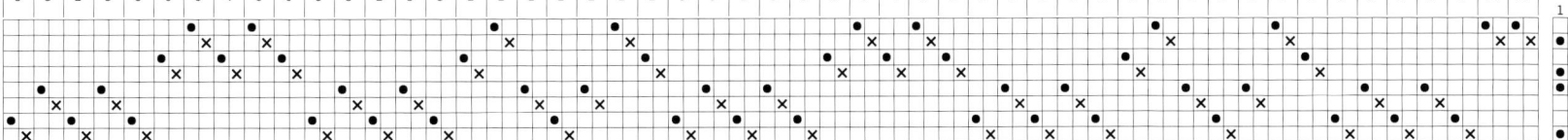

center

A U5 Loden / U49 Larch Green
B U7 Oak / U43 Beige
C U91 Flaxon
D U77 Dusty Coral / S768 Clay
E S2 Black / U25 Medium Brown
F U75 Cobalt / U47 Charcoal
G U18 Copen / U95 Mineral
H U77 Dusty Coral / U128 Quince

Warp Sequence

A	184	26	6	4	6	6	12	4	12	6	6	4	6	6	12	32	12	6	6	4	6	6	12	4	12	6	6	4	6	6
B		26		4		6					6		4		6				6		4		6					6		4	6
C			6		6			4		6			6					6		6		4			6		6			
D																															
E							12		12															12		12					
F																32															
G															12		12														
H																															

edge

A	12	32	12	6	6	4	6	6	12	4	12	6	6	4	6	6	12	16	1192
B				6		4		6					6		4		6		232
C					6		6			4				6		6			168
D		32																	64
E									12		12								144
F																		16	96
G																	12		72
H	12		12																48
																	center->		2016

Garden Sofa Pillows & Rug

The *Patchwork* pattern in the subtle tone-on-tone greens brings this textile back to its traditional roots. The big motif really stands out against the colorful small-scale design of the seat cushion fabric. This pattern is easy to thread because the dark green background color is always threaded on the odd shaft and the pattern color goes on the even shaft. The fabric doesn't have the horizontal green border, so it can be woven on 8 treadles. For contrast, some pillows have a dark green background while others are made on the reverse side with a light green background.

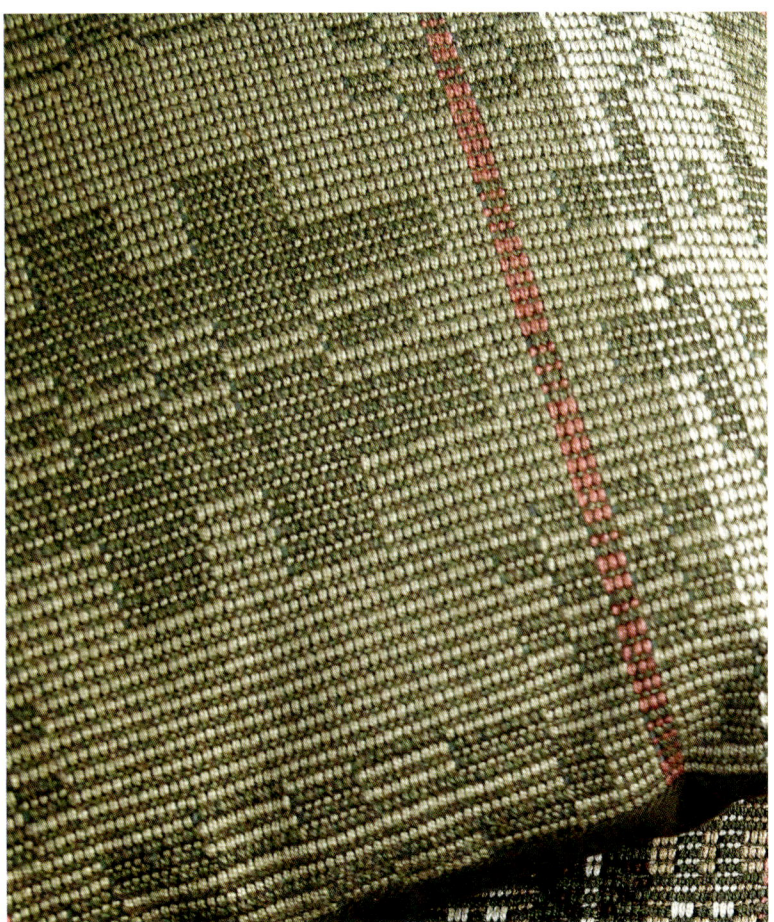

DESIGN *Patchwork*

TECHNIQUE Warp-faced Rep weave, 8 shafts and 10 treadles
If you only have 8 treadles, you can retie the tie-up for treadles 9 and 10 onto treadles 1 and 2 for the top and bottom green border. Or, you can just eliminate the border.

FINISHED SIZE 42" x 42" rug, 36" fabric for pillows or upholstery, 12' warp

MATERIALS See color chart in back for exact project color quantities.

WARP 5/2 pearl cotton, rug and fabric, 12' warp.

WEFT Rug: Thick 200 yards, 8/16MB unmercerized cotton black triple stranded. Thin 300 yards 10/2 pearl cotton black. Fabric: Thick 266 yards, 8/8MB unmercerized cotton or 4/4 cotton. Thin 10/2 pearl cotton 266 yards black.

REED 12-dent reed, 4 ends per dent, 2 ends per heddle

SETT 48 ends per inch

WIDTH IN REED 42" (less 4 ends)

WEFT SETT Rug: 17 rows (thick and thin) =5",
Fabric: 30 rows (thick and thin) = 5"

NUMBER OF ENDS 2012

WEAVING Whether weaving a rug or fabric, start with thick as you alternate thick and thin weft. Weave the top and bottom border to the same size as the solid green side borders. For the 42" rug, you will use 3 pattern repeats and weave to 48" plus 3" each hem. For the fabric, weave to 38", no hem, border optional.

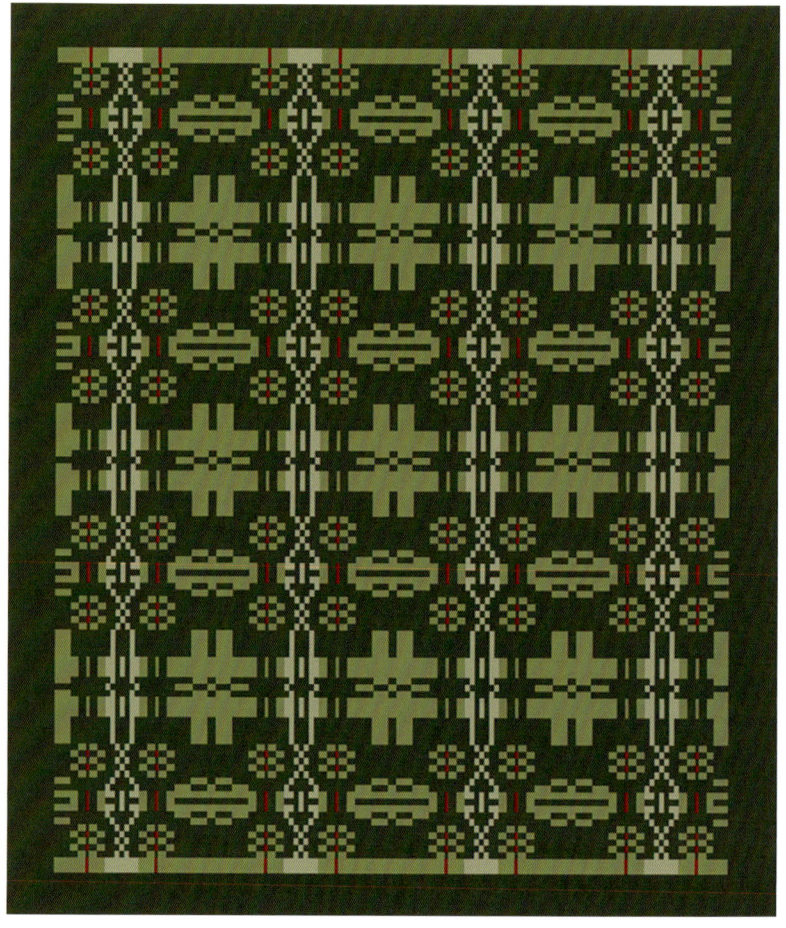

Rug pattern

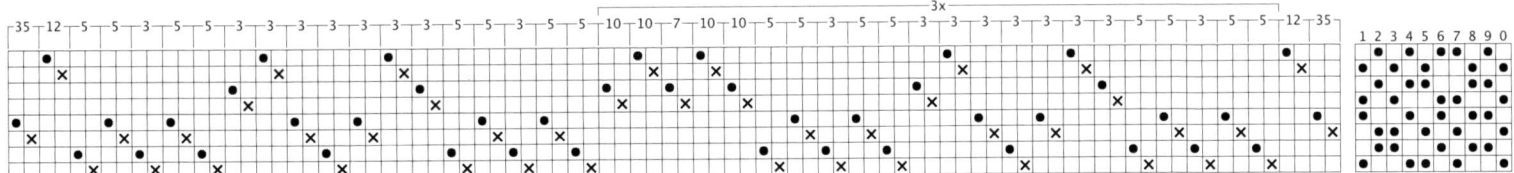

2 ends per heddle

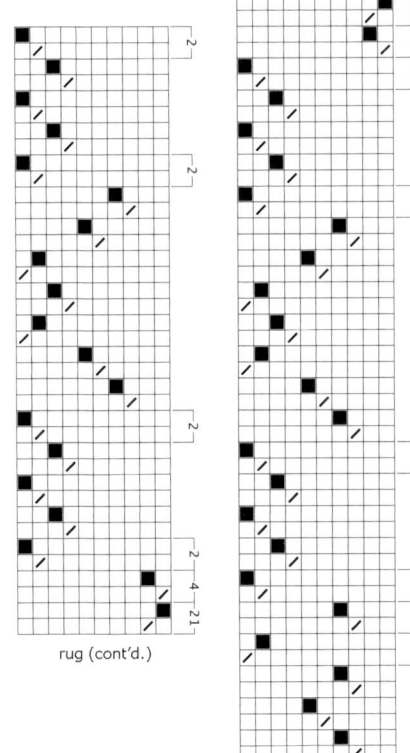

rug (cont'd.)

rug

fabric

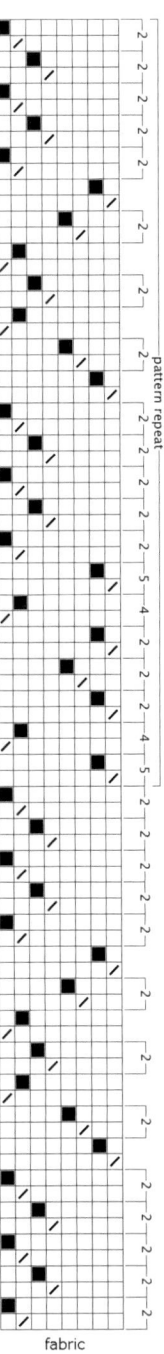

Warp Sequence

A U5 Loden Green / U49 Larch Green
B S38 Dill
C S42 Hemp / U91 Flaxon
D U77 Dusty Coral / S768 Clay

			Repeat 3x															
A	140	24	20	6	20	42	20	6	114	20	6	20	42	20	6	44	140	1146
B		24	20		20		20		114	20		20		20		44		650
C						42							42					168
D				6				6			6				6			48
																		2012

Garden Room Red Sofa & Pillows

This sweet little sofa was quite the find at a second hand store. It beckoned for a custom designed fabric, so I indulged with the green stripe centered on the back cushion of the sofa which continues all the way around to the backside as well. With the wide expanse of the *Oleana* design, the circles cluster to create rose motifs in the red area. There are endless possibilities with this design, so try playing with it on the computer or graph paper and see how many variations you can make.

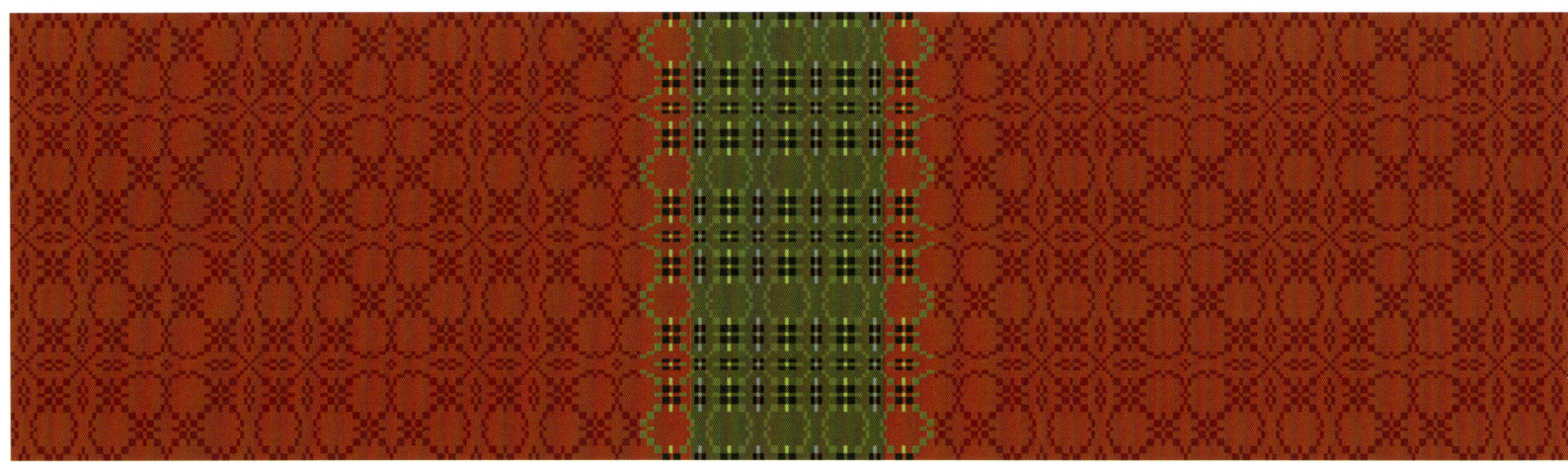

DESIGN *Oleana*

TECHNIQUE   Warp-faced Rep weave, 8 shafts and 8 treadles

FINISHED SIZE   71" x 2 yards. (15 yards for the 54" x 36" sofa)

MATERIALS   See color chart in back for exact project color quantities.

WARP   5/2 pearl cotton, 11' warp yields 2 yards of fabric

WEFT   Thick 900 yards 8/8MB umercerized cotton or 4/4 cotton black. Thin 900 yards 10/2 pearl cotton black.

REED   12-dent reed, 4 ends per dent, 2 ends per heddle

SETT   48 ends per inch

WIDTH IN REED   71.16"

WEFT SETT   30 rows (thick and thin) = 5"

NUMBER OF ENDS   3416

WEAVING   The threading draft depicts the pattern from the beginning to the center. You will need to reverse the threading order from the center continuing to the other edge while maintaining odd/even alternations of shafts. The background colors A and C are always on the even numbered shafts and the pattern colors are threaded on the odd numbered shafts. Start with thick as you alternate thick and thin weft. Weave to 76" for two yards of fabric.

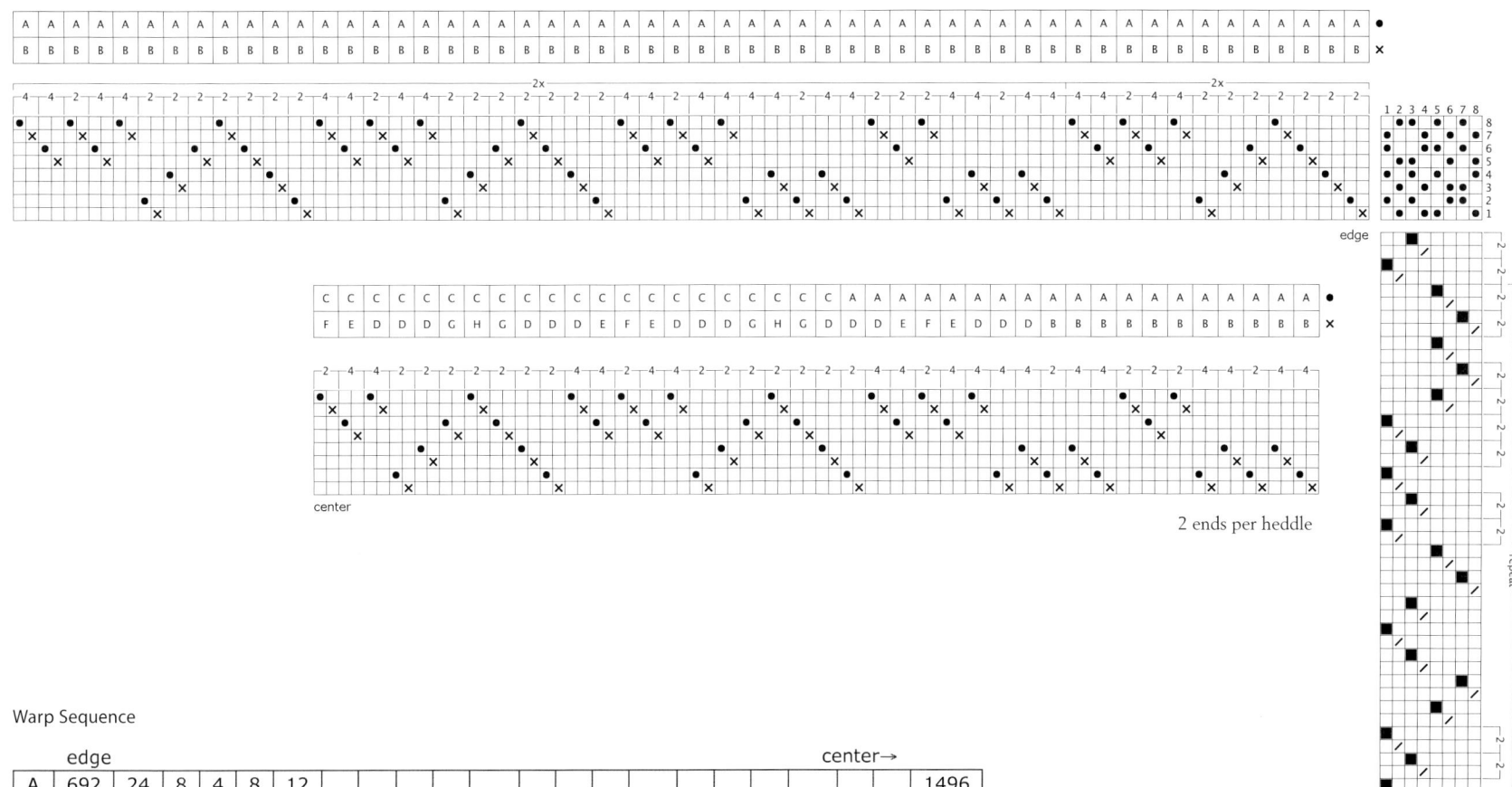

Warp Sequence

	edge																center→	
A	692	24	8	4	8	12												1496
B	692																	1384
C							4	4	4	4	16	8	4	8	16	4	4	4	16	8	4	212
D		24			12	4			16			16			16		176
E		8		8					8		8				8		80
F			4							4						4	20
G					4		4					4	4				32
H							4						4				16
																	3416

- **A** U149 Burnt Orange / U32 Lipstick
- **B** U17 Wine / U24 Garnet
- **C** U87 Verdant
- **D** U50 Avocado
- **E** U49 Larch Green
- **F** U152 Pistachio / S105 Chartreuse
- **G** U34 Maroon
- **H** U134 Cactus / U68 King Blue

Garden Room Curtain & Throw

The perfect complement to the *Patchwork* rug, this curtain is woven in the same sumptuous fabric as the throws. This mostly two-toned design is a bit subdued with just a touch of the bold green color on the border, but the garnet red will still knock your socks off.

DESIGN *Oleana*

TECHNIQUE Balanced Thick-and-Thin, 8 shafts and 8 treadles
FINISHED SIZE 46" x 84", 1 curtain panel or 1 throw
MATERIALS See color chart in back for exact project color quantities.
WARP 5/2 pearl cotton, 13' warp for one curtain panel
WEFT Thick 770 yards 3/2 pearl cotton U17 Wine. Thin 20/2 pearl cotton 890 yards black.
REED 10-dent reed, 2 ends per dent, one thread per heddle
SETT 20 ends per inch
WIDTH IN REED 50.6"
WEFT SETT 29 rows (thick and thin) = 5"
NUMBER OF ENDS 1012

WEAVING When you tie the warp onto the back beam, distribute the extra 12 ends across the width of the warp. Start weaving with thick as you alternate thick and thin weft. Weave the throw to 92" plus 3" each hem. Add extra hem to the curtain if desired.

A double fly-shuttle will really speed up the weaving. When using the fly-shuttle, it works best to thread the two ends at each selvage in a tabby using a separate pair of shafts. This way the edge threads are always catching so the weft thread does not pull back into the weaving. Machine wash in warm water and dry to full the fabric. It is best to line the curtain to prevent fading and deterioration from the sun. When using the fabric as a curtain, you can expect it to stretch 2-3 inches in length over time.

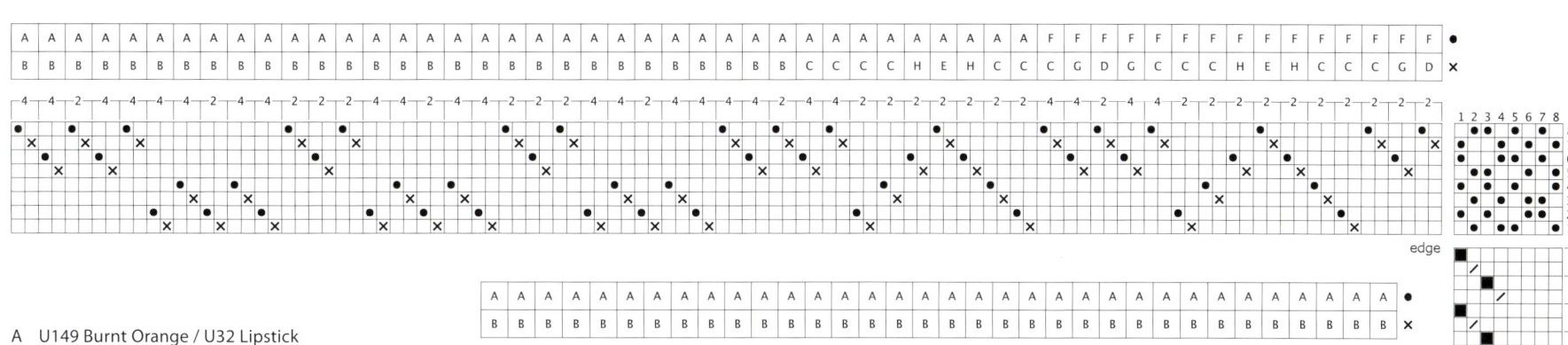

- A U149 Burnt Orange / U32 Lipstick
- B U17 Wine / U24 Garnet
- C U50 Avocado
- D U152 Pistachio / S105 Chartreuse
- E U134 Cactus / U68 King Blue
- F U87 Verdant
- G U49 Larch Green
- H U34 Maroon

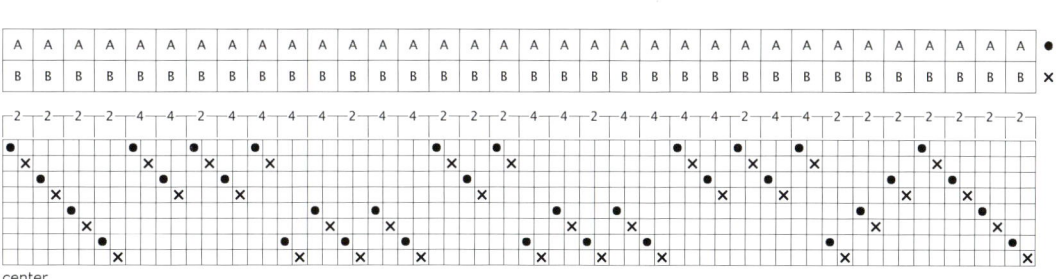

Single ends threaded through the heddles

Warp Sequence

A							4	2	2	2	12	386	12	2	2	2	4					430
B												386										386
C		6		8		4	4			12		12		4	4			8		6		68
D	2			2													2				2	8
E		2					2			2				2				2				8
F	2	2	6	2	2	8	4	2	4	4				4	4	2	8	2	2	2	6	2	2	76
G		2			4	4								4		4				2		20
H			2		2			2		2				2		2			2		2		16
																							1012

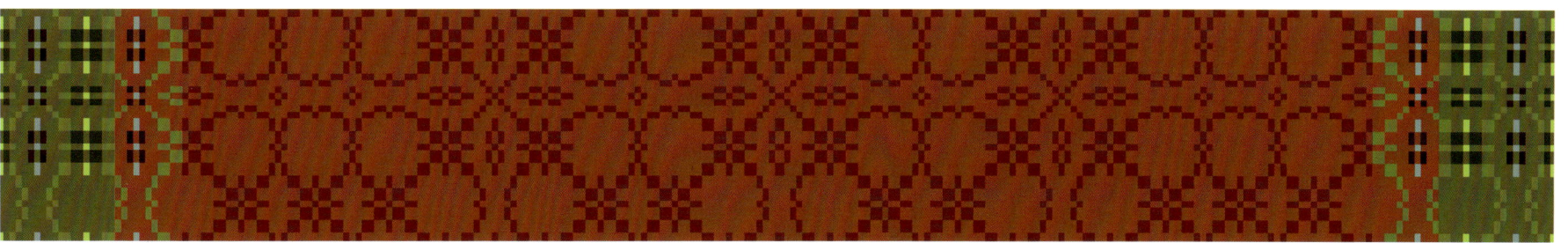

109

Garden Room Throw

The *Waterdance* throw encompasses all the colors of the *Oleana* sofa plus brings in a gold and orange from the nearby *Patchwork* rug. The colorful block pattern is a modern but fitting accompaniment to the delicate pattern in the sofa and the bold traditional pattern in the rug.

DESIGN *Waterdance*

TECHNIQUE   Balanced Thick-and Thin, 10 shafts and 10 treadles

FINISHED SIZE   46" x 84" throw

MATERIALS   See color chart in back for exact project color quantities.

WARP   5/2 pearl cotton, 13' warp

WEFT   Thick 770 yards 3/2 pearl cotton U87 verdant. Thin 890 yards 20/2 pearl cotton black.

REED   10-dent, 2 ends per dent, one thread per heddle

SETT   20 ends per inch

WIDTH IN REED   50"

WEFT SETT   29 rows (thick and thin) = 5"

NUMBER OF ENDS   1000

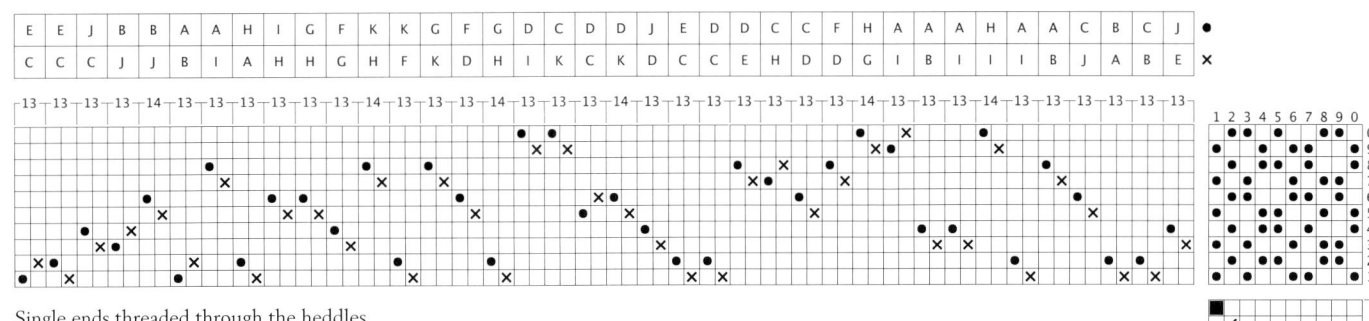

Single ends threaded through the heddles

WEAVING   Start weaving with thick as you alternate thick and thin weft. Weave the throw to 92" plus 3" each hem. A double fly-shuttle will really speed up the weaving. When using the fly-shuttle, it works best to thread the last 2 ends at each selvage in a tabby using a separate pair of shafts. This way the edge threads are always catching so the weft thread does not pull back into the weaving. Machine wash in warm water and dry to full the fabric.

- **A** U149 Burnt Orange / U32 Lipstick
- **B** U17 Wine / U24 Garnet
- **C** U87 Verdant
- **D** U50 Avocado
- **E** U49 Larch Green
- **F** U152 Pistachio / S105 Chartreuse
- **G** U7 Oak / U89 California Gold
- **H** U108 Light Rust
- **I** U149 Burnt Orange
- **J** U34 Maroon
- **K** U134 Cactus/ W2166 Porcelain Blue

Warp Sequence

A		13		13	13		13	13	13															13	13	13		117
B		13	13		13			13																		13	27		92
C		13		13							13	13		13	13		13	13									13	26	143
D									13	13			13	13		13	14	13		13		13							118
E	13										13		13															26	65
F								13											13		13		13						52
G								14										14		13			13	13					67
H				14				14		13								14			14		13	13	13				108
I					13	14	13		13							13								13		13			92
J	13		13										13													27	13		79
K															14		13			13	13	14							67
																													1000

Porch Table Runner & Placemats

This square pattern looks so simple, yet it is not just a simple square pattern. It is the color blending and multiple shafts and treadles that make this pattern shimmer and move in an irregular fashion. Try even more treadles if you have them!

DESIGN *Waterdance*

TECHNIQUE   Warp-faced Rep weave, 10 shafts and 10 treadles

FINISHED SIZE   table runner 13 x 40", 6 placemats 13" x 18" each

MATERIALS   See color chart in back for exact project color quantities.

WARP   5/2 pearl cotton, table runner and 6 placemats, 19' warp

WEFT   Thick 338 yards 8/16MB unmercerized cotton black. Thin 367 yards 10/2 pearl cotton black.

REED   12-dent reed, 4 ends per dent, 2 ends per heddle

SETT   48 epi

WIDTH IN REED   13"

WEFT SETT   48 rows (thick and thin) = 8"

NUMBER OF ENDS   624

WEAVING   Start with thick as you alternate thick and thin weft. Weave the runner to 42" plus 2½" each hem. Weave each placemat to 19". Start and end each placemat with ½" of warp for fringe and weave 3 rows of thin weft. To finish, machine sew along last thin weft. To finish the runner, double fold the hem and machine sew next to the first thick pattern shot.

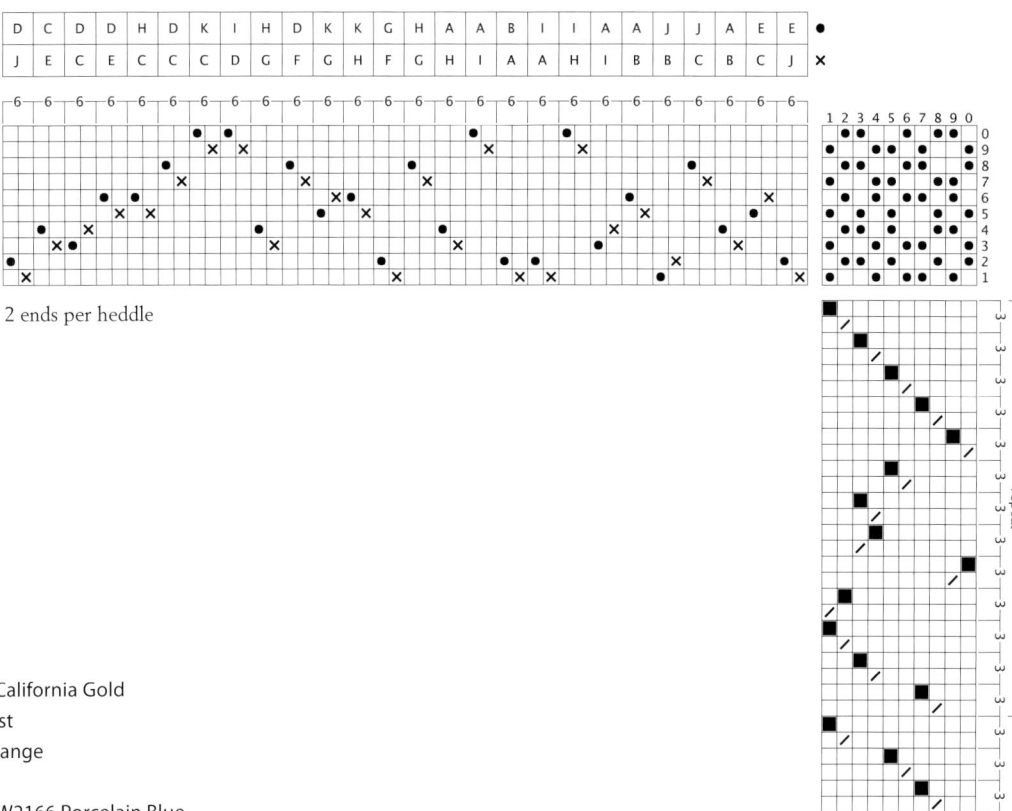

2 ends per heddle

- **A** U149 Burnt Orange / U32 Lipstick
- **B** U17 Wine / U24 Garnet
- **C** U87 Verdant
- **D** U50 Avocado
- **E** U49 Larch Green
- **F** U152 Pistachio / S105 Chartreuse
- **G** U7 Oak / U89 California Gold
- **H** U108 Light Rust
- **I** U149 Burnt Orange
- **J** U34 Maroon
- **K** U134 Cactus / W2166 Porcelain Blue

Warp Sequence

A			12			12	12		12	12	12	12									84
B				12		12	12				12										48
C		12		12										12	12	12		12	12		84
D													12		12		12	12	12	12	72
E	12	12																12	12		48
F										12		12									24
G									12	12		12		12							48
H						12			12	12		12			12		12				72
I					12	12	12		12					12							60
J	12			12	12															12	48
K											12	12			12						36
																					624

Project Color Charts

Pinwheel — Throw 12' warp, Spread 23' warp, add more for pillows

COLOR	ENDS throw/spread	OUNCES throw/spread
U53 Scarab	170/170	5.12/9.92
U87 Verdant	29/29	1/1.76
S294 Quince	50/50	1.6/2.88
W5604 Willow	91/91	2.72/5.28
S105 Chartreuse	12/12	.32/.64
U45 Nile Green	12/12	.32/.64
U94 Tyrol	256/256	7.04/13.6
U95 Mineral	80/80	2.4/4.64
U134 Cactus	32/32	1/1.92
U25 Medium Brown	24/12	.8/.64
U145 Bark	60/30	1.76/1.76
U77 Dusty Coral	24/12	.8/.64
U108 Light Rust	24/12	.8/.64
W7453 Amber Gold	50/25	1.6/1.6
S712 Beechnut	28/14	.8/.8
U122 Mead	78/39	2.4/2.24
U46 Champagne	22/11	.64/.64
W7129 Golden Ocher	42/21	1.28/1.28
TOTAL	1084/908	2.02/3.22 lbs.

Waterdance — Bedroom Table Runner, 10' warp

COLOR	ENDS	OUNCES
U53 Scarab	36	1
S42 Hemp	36	1
S103 Tunisian Teal	60	1.52
U134 Cactus	60	1.52
U98 Mountain	48	1.22
W2574 Heather	12	0.3
U46 Champagne	6	0.23
U140 Safari	6	0.23
S326 Antelope	36	1
S109 Khaki	30	0.76
U108 Light Rust	30	0.76
U149 Burnt Orange	78	2
S91 Tobacco	42	1.07
S143 Burgundy	36	1
U122 Mead	36	1
U119 Hummingbird	36	1
U146 Periwinkle	18	0.46
U126 Denim	18	0.46
TOTAL		1.03 lbs.

Brunch — 3 Dishtowels, 13' warp

COLOR	ENDS	OUNCES
MB5069 Chamois	81	1.6
MB1451 Ivoire	81	1.6
MB5212 Honey	60	1.23
MB1183 Cannelle	60	1.23
MB5213 Cayenne	14	0.29
MB8115 Stone	28	0.58
MB1934 Vertnil	26	0.54
MB4269 Limette pale	26	0.54
MB112 Slate	26	0.54
MB94 Vieux bleu	26	0.54
TOTAL	428	8.69oz

Oleana — Bedroom Rug & Pillows 17' warp

COLOR	ENDS	OUNCES
U77 Dusty Coral	4	0.17
U128 Quince	4	0.17
U149 Burnt Orange	106	4.58
U32 Lipstick	106	4.58
W5604 Willow Green	140	6.04
U87 Verdant	158	6.82
U49 Larch Green	18	0.78
U95 Mineral	82	3.54
U94 Tyrol	82	3.54
U46 Champagne	6	0.26
U7 Oak	6	0.26
U122 Mead	78	3.37
U145 Bark	124	5.35
U25 Medium Brown	46	2
TOTAL		2.59 lbs.

Pinwheel — Kitchen Rugs & Fabric, 20' warp

COLOR	ENDS	OUNCES
U77 Dusty Coral	168	8.53
U108 Light Rust	288	14.63
W7198 Burnt Sienna	88	4.47
S91 Tobacco	32	1.63
U149 Burnt Orange	48	2.44
U34 Maroon	96	4.88
S77 Brick	48	2.44
U119 Hummingbird	128	6.5
u122 Mead	112	5.69
U145 Bark	80	4.06
U87 Verdant	384	19.5
U106 Persian Green	48	2.44
U50 Avocado	112	5.69
S103 Tunisian Teal	80	4.06
U103 Peacock	80	4.06
U48 Dark Turk	32	1.63
U98 Mountain Green	112	5.69
U49 Larch Green	112	5.69
S109 Khaki	32	1.63
U62 Moss Green	32	1.63
TOTAL		6.71 lbs.

Conservatory — Bathroom Rug, 9' warp

COLOR	ENDS	OUNCES
S91 Tobacco	160	3.65
U87 Verdant	120	2.74
S109 Khaki	64	1.46
S38 Dill	458	5.23
U106 Persian Green	85	1.94
W5604 Willow Green	89	2.03
U30 Antique	17	0.39
U43 Beige	87	1.99
S772 Harvest	16	0.37
U68 King Blue	48	1.1
U134 Cactus	48	1.1
U20 Dark Grey	20	0.46
S128 Wedgewood	20	0.46
U78 Charcoal	104	2.38
U15 Navy	104	2.38
TOTAL	1440	2.06 lbs.

Beyond — Living Room Rug, 10' warp

COLOR	ENDS	OUNCES
S38 Dill	169	4.29
U49 Larch	69	1.75
S77 Brick	69	1.75
U99 Dark Sierra	69	1.75
U46 Champagne	24	0.6
U7 Oak	24	0.6
U87 Verdant	14	0.36
S109 Khaki	14	0.36
S42 Hemp	76	1.93
U43 Beige	482	12.24
U25 Medium Brown	182	4.62
S2 Black	68	1.72
U108 Light Rust	54	1.37
W7129 Golden Ochre	54	1.37
U106 Persian Green	24	0.6
TOTAL	**1392**	**2.21 lbs.**

Evolve — Entry Rug, 10' warp

COLOR	ENDS	OUNCES
S103 Tunisian Teal	206	5.23
U134 Cactus	40	1.01
U53 Scarab	89	2.26
S38 Dill	143	3.63
U106 Persian Green	54	1.37
U62 Moss Green	137	3.48
U87 Verdant	137	3.48
U122 Mead	35	0.89
W7129 Golden Ochre	75	1.9
U43 Beige	98	2.49
U139 Chamois	39	0.99
U46 Champagne	25	0.63
U89 California Gold	84	2.13
U107 melon	49	1.24
W7198 Burnt Sienna	153	3.89
S91 Tobacco	100	2.54
U108 Light Rust	104	2.64
S77 Brick	60	1.52
U99 Dark Sierra	50	1.27
U34 Maroon	50	1.27
TOTAL	**1728**	**2.72 lbs.**

Patchwork — Garden Sofa Fabric & Rug, 11' warp

COLOR	ENDS	OUNCES
U5 Loden	596	16.65
U49 Larch	596	16.65
U7 Oak	116	3.24
U43 Beige	116	3.24
U91 Flaxon	168	4.69
U77 Dusty Coral	56	1.56
S768 Clay	32	0.89
S2 Black	72	2.01
U25 Medium Brown	72	2.01
U75 Cobalt	48	1.34
U47 Charcoal	48	1.34
U18 Copen	36	1
U95 Mineral	36	1
U128 Quince	24	0.67
TOTAL	**2016**	**3.52 lbs.**

Conservatory — Dining Room Table Runner & Placemats, 19' warp

COLOR	ENDS	OUNCES
S357 Clay	29	1.4
U122 Mead	29	1.4
U77 Dusty Coral	25	1.2
U108 Light Rust	41	1.98
U61 Topaz	16	0.77
U139 Chamois	16	0.77
U84 Gold Dust	63	3.04
U140 Safari	10	0.48
S42 Hemp	79	3.81
S38 Dill	26	1.25
U134 Cactus	58	2.8
U49 Larch Green	117	5.65
S109 Khaki	20	0.97
U87 Verdant	58	2.8
U8 Evergreen	21	1.01
S2 Black	16	0.77
TOTAL	**624**	**1.88 lbs.**

Patchwork — Garden Room Blue Rug, 9' warp

COLOR	ENDS	OUNCES
U103 Peacock	769	17.58
U98 Mountain	769	17.58
U122 Mead	314	7.18
U29 Old Gold	18	0.41
W7453 Amber Gold	18	0.41
W5604 Willow Green	240	5.48
U87 Verdant	144	3.29
U62 Moss Green	144	3.29
S77 Brick	234	5.35
U24 Garnet	124	2.83
U149 Burnt Orange	110	2.51
TOTAL	**2884**	**4.12 lbs.**

Patchwork — Garden Sofa Pillows, 12' warp

COLOR	ENDS	OUNCES
U5 Loden	573	17.46
U49 Larch	573	17.46
S38 Dill	650	19.8
S42 Hemp	84	2.56
U91 Flaxon	84	2.56
U77 Dusty Coral	24	0.73
S768 Clay	24	0.73
TOTAL	**2012**	**3.83 lbs.**

Oleana — Garden Room Red Rug, 9' warp

COLOR	ENDS	OUNCES
U49 Burnt Orange	280	6.4
U32 Lipstick	280	6.4
U17 Wine	212	4.85
U24 Garnet	212	4.85
U87 Verdant	156	3.56
U50 Avocado	176	4.2
U49 Larch Green	72	1.65
U152 Pistachio	8	0.18
S105 Chartreuse	8	0.18
U34 Maroon	24	0.55
U134 Cactus	6	0.14
U94 Tyrol	6	0.14
TOTAL	1440	2.07 lbs.

Oleana — Garden Room Curtain, 13' warp

COLOR	ENDS	OUNCES
U149 Burnt Orange	215	7.1
U32 Lipstick	215	7.1
U17 Wine	193	6.37
U24 Garnet	193	6.37
U87 Verdant	68	2.25
U50 Avocado	4	0.13
U152 Pistachio	4	0.13
S105 Chartreuse	4	0.13
U134 Cactus	4	0.13
U68 King Blue	76	2.51
U34 Maroon	20	0.66
U49 Larch Green	16	0.53
TOTAL	1012	2.09 lbs.

Waterdance — Porch Table Runner & Placemats, mats 19' warp

COLOR	ENDS	OUNCES
U149 Burnt Orange	102	4.92
U32 Lipstick	48	2.32
U17 Wine	24	1.16
U24 Garnet	24	1.16
U87 Verdant	84	4.05
U50 Avocado	72	3.47
U152 Pistachio	12	0.58
S105 Chartreuse	12	0.58
U7 Oak	24	1.16
U89 California Gold	24	1.16
U108 Light Rust	72	3.47
U134 Cactus	18	0.87
U68 King Blue	18	0.87
U34 Maroon	48	2.32
U49 Larch Green	48	2.32
TOTAL	624	1.9 lbs.

Oleana — Garden Room Red Sofa Fabric, 15' warp

COLOR	ENDS	OUNCES
U149 Burnt Orange	748	20.89
U32 Lipstick	748	20.89
U17 Wine	692	19.33
U24 Garnet	692	19.33
U87 Verdant	212	5.92
U50 Avocado	176	4.91
U152 Pistachio	10	0.28
S105 Chartreuse	10	0.28
U134 Cactus	8	0.22
U68 King Blue	8	0.22
U34 Maroon	32	0.89
U49 Larch Green	80	2.23
TOTAL	3416	5.96 lbs.

Waterdance — Garden Room Throw, 13' warp

COLOR	ENDS	OUNCES
U149 Burnt Orange	151	4.98
U32 Lipstick	59	1.95
U17 Wine	46	1.52
U24 Garnet	46	1.52
U87 Verdant	143	4.72
U50 Avocado	119	3.93
U152 Pistachio	26	0.86
S105 Chartreuse	26	0.86
U7 Oak	33	1.09
U89 California Gold	33	1.09
U108 Light Rust	108	3.57
U134 Cactus	34	1.12
U68 King Blue	34	1.12
U34 Maroon	79	2.61
U49 Larch Green	65	2.15
TOTAL	1002	2.07 lbs.

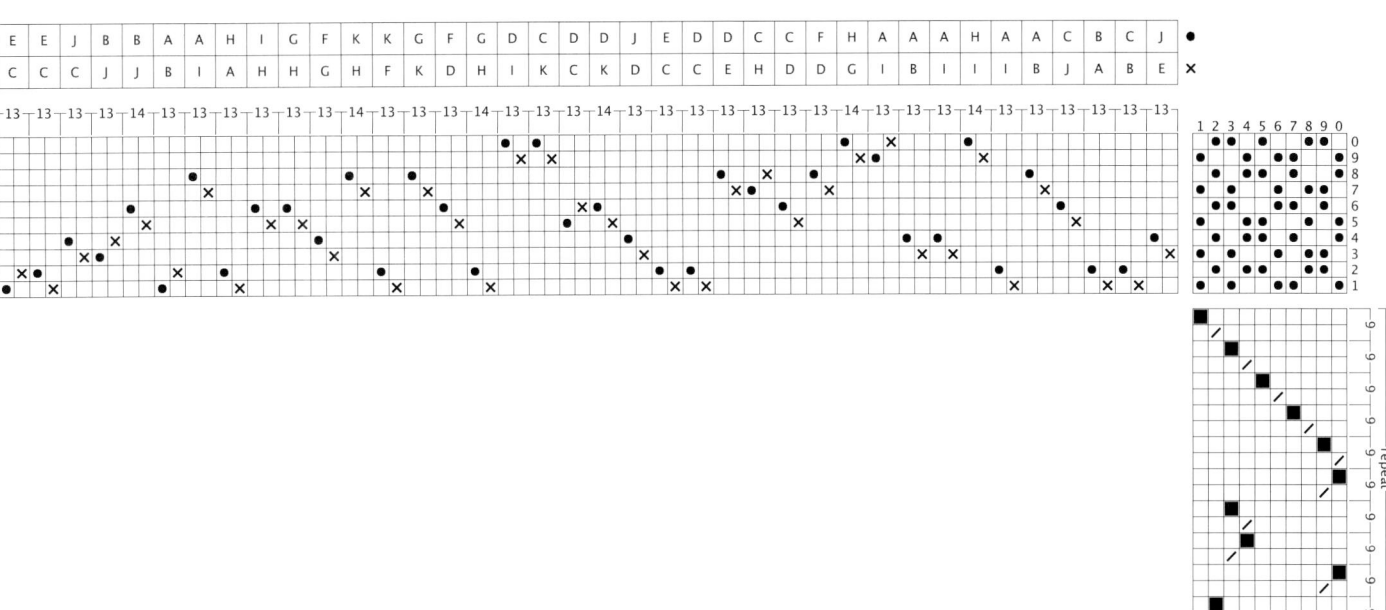

How to Read the Threading Draft

The threading draft and color charts are fairly standard, but I thought a little explanation might be helpful. The letters you see above the draft refer to the color order when threading—note x or dot at the beginning of each row of letters. Each x and each dot in the draft represent two threads threaded through one heddle on one shaft, unless otherwise stated. There is always a pair of adjacent shafts in each column—x on one shaft, dot on the other.

The numbers above the draft refer to the number of heddles required for each of the shafts in the pair. The two threads represented by each symbol (x or dot) are multiplied by the number above the column to give you the total number of threads on that shaft in the column. You will find this helpful when planning your project and calculating the number of heddles you will need on the loom. You will notice that Rep weave requires a lot of heddles. Reading left to right, the warp color chart shows the total number of threads for each color on each shaft.

Calculating Warp and Weft

It is always fun to have lots of colors on the shelf to play with but when it comes down to it, you need to make sure you have enough yarn to complete your project. First, you will want to figure out the length of the warp. To do this, take the woven length of the piece including the hems, add 20% for shrinkage and another 12–36" for loom waste. This will be the length of your warp. Now to figure out the amount of warp for each color; add up the number of ends using a specific color, multiple that number by the length of the warp in feet, divide by 3 (yards), then divide by 2100 for 5/2 pearl cotton (number of yards/pound). This will give you the number of pounds of yarn you need for that color. If you want to figure out how many ounces you will need, take the number of pounds you have and multiply it by 16 and that will tell you the number of ounces you need for that color. Repeat this process for each color.

For the weft you can estimate the pics per inch for the different woven weights as follows:

Heavy rug weight – 17 rows (thick and thin) = 5"
Medium table runner weight – 48 rows (thick and thin) = 8"
Fabric weight – 30 rows (thick and thin) = 5"
Blanket weight – 29 rows (thick and thin) = 5"
Dishtowel weight – 41 rows (thick and thin) = 5"

Table runners

Rugs and throws

Yarn Sources

The yarn code refers to the company that carries specific colors on the project color charts.

Maurice Brassard Fils Inc. (code MB)
1573 Savoie C.P. 4-Plessisville Que
Canada G6L2Y6
www.mbrassard.com / 819-362-2408
- 8/2 unmercerized cotton 3360 yds/lb
  – dishtowel warp
- 8/8 unmercerized cotton 840 yds/lb
  – thick weft upholstery, pillows, tote
- 8/16 unmercerized cotton 420 yds/lb
  – thick weft placemats, table runners
    use triple stranded for rug weft

Silk City Fibers (code S)
155 Oxford St.
Paterison, NJ 07522
www.silkcityfibers.com / 800-899-7455
- 3/2, 5/2, 10/2 pearl cotton

UKI Supreme Corporation (code U)
325 Spencer Rd.
Conover, NC 28613
www.ukisupreme.com / 888-604-6975
- 3/2 pearl cotton 1260 yds/lb – blanket thick weft
- 5/2 pearl cotton 2100 yds/lb – Rep weave and blanket warp
- 10/2 pearl cotton 4200 yds/lb – thin weft Rep weave
- 20/2 pearl cotton 8400 yds/lb – thin weft Thick-and-Thin technique

Yarn Barn
930 Massachusetts St.
Lawrence, KS 66044
www.yarnbarn-ks.com | 800-468-0035
- UKI 3/2, 5/2, 10/2, 20/2 pearl cotton
- MB 8/2-B, 8/16 heavy cotton, unmercerized cotton

Webs (code W)
75 Service Center Rd.
Northampton, MA 01060
www.yarn.com / 800-367-9327
- 5/2 pearl cotton – Rep weave warp

I Love Yarn
401 Egrep Circle
Delrey Beach, FL 33444
www.iloveyarn.com / 845-452-8408
- 4/4 unmercerized cotton 850 yds/lb thick weft upholstery, pillows, tote, available in black and natural

Weavers Guild of MN
3000 University Ave. #101
St. Paul, MN 55414
www.weaversguildmn.org / 612-436-0463
- UKI 3/2, 5/2, 10/2 pearl cotton
- MB 8/2 unmercerized cotton

The Village Spinning & Weaving Shop
425 Alisal Rd.
Solvang, CA 93463-3704
www.villagespinweave.com / 805-686-1192
- pearl and unmercerized cotton

Acknowledgments

Thank you to all our patrons, weavers, and supporters who value the fiber arts and bring them into their environments.

Thank you to my entire family and friends, especially, Chris Hall, Coya Hall, Susan Anderson Kimm, Barry Kimm, Colleen Marshall. Without your support and encouragement this work would not be possible.

To Neva Conway and Trisha Malin, and our talented weavers—without you this work would not exist. Thank you to Sue Fairchild, Mary Skoy, Adam Demers, Karen Searle, Marcia Anderson, Margaret Miller, Lila Nelson, Paula Pfaff, and MRAC.

A special thank you to Dyan Richardson for planting the seed to write this book, to Amy Egenberger for bringing this dream to life, and to John Abernathy for making my vision possible for all to see.

About the Author

Kelly Marshall, designer and weaver, is the founder of Custom Woven Interiors, a business specializing in creating textiles for residential and corporate settings. She is recognized for the welcoming color, pattern, and Rep weave technique that characterize her weavings.

Her award-winning textiles have been exhibited at the finest national craft shows including The Smithsonian and The Philadelphia Museum of Art Craft Show. Marshall is featured on Modern Masters and MN Original television series, and in publications such as *Home & Garden, Midwest Home, Mpls. St. Paul* and *Arts & Crafts Home*. Kelly Marshall lives and keeps her studio in Minneapolis, Minnesota.

Copyright © 2012 Kelly Marshall
Photographs copyright © 2012 John Abernathy

Copy Editor: Mary Skoy
Draft Editor: Sue Fairchild — PixeLoom software
Designer: Adam Demers
Additional photography credits go to:
Peter Lee — *Urban* pg 23, *Pinwheel* pg 21, *Flash* pg 21, *Wright* pg 12, *Patchwork* pg 14, *Traditions* pg 13.
Jeffery Howe — FLW Hollyhock House pg 10.
Garnet Hill & Christopher Hubble — rug photo pg 17.

Printed in Canada

Library of Congress Control Number: 2012903412

ISBN 978-0-9852071-0-6

All rights reserved. No portion of this book may be reproduced, by any means, without written permission from the publisher, except by a reviewer quoting brief excerpts for the purpose of review. Weave designs in this book are copyright © Custom Woven Interiors Ltd. and are for personal use only, not to be produced for resale.

Published by Custom Woven Interiors Ltd.
1500 Jackson St. NE #386, Minneapolis, MN 55413
Orders: 612-788-7800
www.kellymarshall.com